Inside the
EISA Computers

TONY DOWDEN

D1716705

Addison-Wesley Publishing Company, Inc.
Reading, Massachusetts   Menlo Park, California   New York
Don Mills, Ontario   Wokingham, England   Amsterdam   Bonn
Sydney   Singapore   Tokyo   Madrid   San Juan

Many of the designations used by manufacturers and sellers to distinguish their products are claimed as trademarks. Where those designations appear in this book and Addison-Wesley was aware of a trademark claim, the designations have been printed in initial capital letters.

Library of Congress Cataloging-in-Publication Data

Dowden, Tony
      Inside the EISA computers / Tony Dowden.
            p.   cm.
      ISBN 0-201-52397-3
      1. EISA (computer bus) 2. Computer architecture. I. Title.
TK7895.B87D69   1990
621.39'16--dc20   90-14
                                                                   CIP

Cover design by Doliber Skeffington
Text design by Total Concept Associates
Set in 11-point Century Schoolbook by Impressions Publishing Services

ISBN 0-201-52397-3
ABCDEFGHIJ-MW-9543210

First Printing, February 1990

This book is dedicated to the hundreds of hard-working engineers in the EISA consortium. They had a challenge: to forge on in the face of adversity and create a new bus, computers, and accessories that can answer the needs of computer users for years to come. They did it.

Acknowledgments

Making acknowledgments in this book is a difficult task, because I am grateful to so many. I can only hope to acknowledge almost everyone and sincerely apologize to anyone I have omitted. None of you will ever be forgotten, and you will always be remembered with gratitude. The list is in no particular order for it is difficult to say that any one did any more than any other. Thanks to:

My wife, Patty, who tolerated the long hours required to do this book. Her suggestions were invaluable; without them this book would be far less than it is.

Gayle Dolby of Hewlett-Packard, who went far out of her way to assist me in securing clearance from the corporate powers to do this book.

Rich Archuletta, who first saw the value of a book like this. It was he who championed it through the EISA consortium, and acted as a buffer from the politics that accompanies an effort of this nature.

Alan VanWinkle and especially Eric Behnke of Hewlett-Packard, programmers of the highest caliber, who provided a great deal of assistance in the software sections of this book.

Jon M. Greenwood and others of Micrografx, Inc. Their contribution of Micrografx Designer version 2.0 allowed me to do the artwork in this book far faster and better than I could have otherwise.

Behind every successful book is a publisher's staff, editors, and assistants, who make the book so much better with their efforts. To Julie Stillman, Carole McClendon, Beth Burleigh, Colleen Jensen, and so many others . . . thanks.

And last but not least, I must acknowledge the assistance of Gato (Attila the Fun), my Maine Coon cat. A gentle giant, he kept me company long after the rest of the family went to bed. It was he who always had praise, showing it with a purr at every opportunity. If only I could get him to sleep someplace other than the top of the laser printer.

Contents

3   The Operating System   31

4   The EISA Bus   55

8   Serial Data Communications   157

9 The Parallel Printer Connector   191

Preface

Today's personal computer is almost a decade old, a quite significant age in a time when changes and new technology pop up overnight, continuously replacing last week's innovations with newer and better innovations. The personal computer is just such a creature, with manufacturers announcing newer and faster versions, seemingly on a weekly basis. Indeed, it is doubtful that anyone can claim to have seen or used one of every model of personal computer that has been marketed in the last ten years.

Through this decade of change, one thing seemed to remain constant—the bus connectors inside the computer where accessory cards could be installed. These accessory cards enhanced the power of the computer, allowing it to use more and more peripherals, contain more memory (RAM and disk drives), and display more lines of more colors.

Over time, the bus went from a single connector with 8 data bits to a double connector with 16 data bits. This allowed more data to flow faster, and with that came the newer 16-bit processors with their faster clock speeds. Finally, IBM decided that the original bus was no longer serviceable and came out with a new computer using their MCA (Micro Channel Architecture) bus. This bus used entirely different connectors and, in fact, had an entirely different concept in accessory card implementation.

However, there were other companies who had large investments in the old bus and were not ready to abandon it. They felt it needed only an enhancement to bring it up to, and perhaps exceed, the performance of the MCA bus. Thus the EISA bus was born, a bus which fulfills the hope of performance exceeding the MCA bus while retaining the ability to use all of the existing cards.

Detractors from the EISA bus were against the enhanced standard, saying it was a "new" standard and the interests of the users would not be well served by yet another standard. The EISA bus is *not* a new standard that renders anything obsolete; it is a significant enhancement of the old standard.

Although this is one of its benefits, it is by no means the most significant benefit. When new computers are announced, there is often a lag of a year or more before significant numbers of expansion cards or compatible software are available for the new computer. With the EISA computer, the announcement of the first computers presents no such problem. Over 1,000 expansion cards are already available that are compatible with the EISA bus!

At the same time, the new EISA computers have room for expansion well beyond their present configurations. They are designed to accommodate processors currently available, such as the Intel 80486, and processors as yet unannounced or even conceived.

In writing this book, I became aware that the first of the EISA computers is not representative of the full power of the bus, but merely an introduction—a glimpse—into the incredible power that EISA-based computers will provide in the next decade.

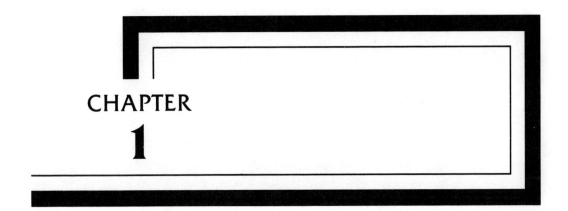

CHAPTER
1

Introduction

Welcome to EISA, the computer architecture "for the rest of us." This book will guide you through the EISA computer from the perspective of a user, an engineer, and a programmer. A lot of information is contained in this book, some of it introductory—for the newcomer, and some of it technical—for the engineer. This book dissects the EISA computer, probing some of its secrets and learning about the source of its power.

And powerful it is. The EISA bus is an enhancement that will serve the computer community for many years, providing the platform upon which to build machines with as yet undreamed of power. It supports Intel processors from the 8086 to the 80486 and beyond. It also supports processors from other sources, such as the Motorola 68000 family. It can even run different processors simultaneously as multiple bus masters, and allow multiple users to simultaneously run different software packages and different operating systems, such as OS/2 and UNIX.

This book is your first step toward understanding the power of the EISA bus and the operation of EISA-based computers. From here, you can move on to learning more about computer architecture, hardware and software, or using applications programs. This book also serves as a basis for understanding the differences in the EISA architecture as offered by different manufacturers.

This book assumes that you have at least a small knowledge of computers. The more you know about computers in general, the easier it will be for you to grasp the concepts presented here. However, if you are a computer novice, you will still get a great deal of understanding and appreciation of the world of EISA.

Throughout this book, you will find terms like "usually" or "typically." I am not trying to be vague—that wouldn't be nice and authors are supposed to be nice. What I am doing, however, is to warn you that although the information presented in that specific area is both typical and accurate, different manufacturers may deviate in an effort to distinguish their equipment from the offerings of other manufacturers.

This book begins with a history of the EISA organization and then turns to an overview of the workings of an EISA computer, both hardware and software. The discussion is of a general nature, and a newcomer to the world of computers should have little trouble with the section. From there it jumps into the heart of the computer with a more technical discussion, revealing the workings of the EISA bus, the operation of associated hardware and software routines, and then on to EISA software. Following that, the loose ends are tied with a discussion of video and peripheral interfaces and the 80486 processor. A glossary, some handy reference tables, and an index round it out. Programming examples are included to help you understand some of the concepts presented, and you are free to use any of them in any way that may help you. Modifications may be required for them to execute on a particular system.

If you are looking for in-depth engineering information, this book is just a starting point. In-depth information can be obtained only from the EISA specification itself (at this time, over 430 pages of detailed and complex information). Note that EISA is not all that complex: the specification is just that complete.

Notation and Conventions

In this book, some forms of notation may be new to you or may not be consistent with what you are accustomed to seeing. They are defined below.

- **Signal names** are shown in their active state. When a signal is active high, it is represented by its mnemonic name. When it is active low, its mnemonic name is followed by a tilde (˜). (This technique allows the computer to sort the names properly on signal name lists.)

  In addition, some signal names may differ from manufacturer to manufacturer. The signal names used here are provided in the EISA specification.

- Some signal lines are **slot specific**. The slot number is shown by a lower case x that, in some references, may be replaced by the number of the slot.

- A **bus name** is identified by its mnemonic name, followed by the range of bits the bus covers enclosed in angle brackets and separated by a colon. For example, D<15:8> covers the data lines from D15 to D8.

- **Program listings** are shown in a fixed-width typeface, and follow the conventions of the Microsoft Assembler.

- **Hexadecimal numbers** are shown with a lowercase letter **h** suffix. Any numbers without the **h** suffix are decimal values.

- **Logic levels** are represented as high (1) or low (0). Specific voltage level equivalents are a function of the source component and should be obtained from the manufacturer's specification sheet.

The History of EISA

On September 13, 1988, a group of computer industry leaders announced that they had joined their engineering forces to create a major enhancement to the ISA (Industry Standard Architecture) bus. This group, a consortium of over 50 leading manufacturers, was led by a core of nine member companies: Hewlett-Packard, Compaq, Zenith, Wyse, Epson, AST, Olivetti, NEC, and Tandy. They called their concept the EISA (Extended Industry Standard Architecture) bus, and provided a full 32-bit enhancement for the 16-bit ISA standard as used in the AT-class computers. In part an answer to the announcement by IBM of their MCA (Micro Channel Architecture), the EISA bus standard was to provide an entirely different approach to the solutions required by the problems of the ISA bus. The ISA bus had served well, but the requirements of the industry, primarily data transfer rates between bus peripherals, could no longer be met by the ISA standard.

IBM's answer to the limitations of the ISA bus was the MCA bus, a complete redesigning of the bus to make it 32 bits, and a redesigning of the computer as a whole. The new IBM computers used the latest technology available at the time, from low-power components to surface-mount components, to offer a series of desktop and deskside computers. A big disadvantage of the new MCA bus was the lack of accessories for the MCA-based machines, something that numbered in the thousands for the old ISA standard.

The companies who announced the new EISA architecture took a very different approach. Their solution to the problem of bus throughput was also to expand the data bus to 32 bits, but they did it using a modified version of the ISA connector. Their modifications essentially added a second row of contacts above the ISA connection pins, and by putting in some blocks to keep the ISA cards from being inserted too far, they could accommodate all of the earlier ISA designs in addition to any of the new 32-bit cards to be provided by members of the consortium or outside vendors.

Among the many advantages cited by the consortium was that all of the expansion cards available at the time were still fully functional in the new computer design. This was often misunderstood, for many of those who questioned the standard thought that the motivation was that people could simply pull the cards out of their old computers and plug them into the new computer. Although this is indeed possible, it is an unlikely possibility. People usually pass on their computers whole to the next owner when they acquire a new computer. The real advantage of the EISA configuration is that, at the time the first EISA computers became available, over 1,000 already existing cards could plug right in and work. This provides complete functionality for any configuration that a user might want, using the components of today. It also provides the basis of an enhanced system using cards that take full advantage of the power of the 32-bit EISA bus. This includes features such as automatic configuration of the cards (no more DIP switches to set), and the power that comes with a 32-bit data bus, such as data transfer rates up to 33MB per second.

After the initial announcement in September, 1988, the industry began buzzing with rumors about the EISA bus, especially the connector. Many magazine articles were written about it, some of them claiming it would be an additional connector in front of the other two original connectors. Others claimed it would be an additional connector next to the original connector. The only ones who were not speculating were the actual engineers working on the connector, and they had something much better in mind. They were working with several connector manufacturers on a design that would provide all the signal lines required, but would require no additional insertion forces, no additional real estate on the mother board, and would provide an increase in reliability. In the end, the Burndy Corporation, a well-known and respected industry leader working with the mechanical engineers, came up with just the right combination of contact designs, connector molding, pin locations, and other factors that made the EISA bus what it is today. Other connector companies will be supplying the connector as well.

The EISA consortium was picking up momentum, and new companies were joining almost daily. In fact, as of this writing, the number of companies on the roster is over 200, and still growing. As each of the new companies joined, they received a copy of the EISA specification and access to any information they required to design computers, accessories, or software for the EISA system. As the specification was refined, updates were sent out to each of the member companies.

At the same time as the connector was being finalized, Intel was busy working on a chip set to complement the EISA bus. The result of their efforts is the 82350 EISA chip set, four integrated circuits that replace most of the components found in the IBM AT-style computers. The EISA chip set was designed to be compatible with both the 80486, the 80386, and the 30386SX CPUs. The 82350 EISA chip set uses CHMOS technology for low power operation and fully supports the ISA bus as well as the EISA bus.

Simultaneously with the development of the connector and the chip set, several of the companies, notably Hewlett-Packard and Compaq, were busy developing the DMA and interrupt concepts and the configuration software. The DMA and interrupt concepts that resulted provided speed and power that were undreamed of in the earlier ISA bus. The configuration software, a package that would eventually find its way into the hands of all developers, was designed to allow each manufacturer to customize it for a particular system. Both of the main software packages that were developed, one for configuring the computer's nonvolatile memory, and one for creating configuration files for accessories, required a great deal of cooperative interaction on the part of Hewlett-Packard and Compaq. The result, however, is a software package that provides all the necessary functionality, and has been translated by the creating companies into a number of foreign languages for the markets in the rest of the world.

On October 10, 1989, Hewlett-Packard announced the first of the EISA computers. Significant in the announcement was not only the 25 MHz 80486 computer, but the fact that the H-P Apollo workstation division would also be using the EISA bus in some of its products. Other announcements followed, and the number of EISA computers keeps growing on a weekly basis.

The result of this historic cooperation is a computer system that is fully compatible among the different manufacturers. And because the specification is the result of cooperation among these companies, the EISA computers represent the best thinking of all these engineering departments, and a stability that comes from an agreement between the top engineering departments of companies who are truly concerned about the needs of their customers.

EISA Providers

Through October 10, 1989, the following companies have publicly stated that they intend to provide EISA products. Of these, there are nine core members, often referred to as the "gang of nine," shown here in bold print. In addition to these companies, there are a number of additional companies (about 50) who prefer to have their names withheld until a future date.

3COM Corporation	**AST Research, Inc.**
ACC Microelectronics Corp.	Atlas Computer Systems
Acer Technology	AT&T Computer Systems
Adaptec, Inc.	Austek Microsystems
Adra Systems, Inc.	Autocomputer Co., Ltd.
Advanced Hardware	Autodesk, Inc.
Architecture	Banyan Systems Inc.
American Megatrends, Inc.	Borland International
Amp, Inc.	Burndy Corporation
Amstrad Plc	Bustek
Apollo Computer, Inc.	Chase Research Limited
Arche Technologies Inc.	Chicony Electronic Co., Ltd.
Arnet Controls, Inc.	Chips & Technologies, Inc.
ASEM S.P.A.	Cirrus Logic, Inc.
Ashton Tate	Clone Computers

Codenoll Technology Corp.
Communication Mach. Corp.
Compaq Computer Corp.
Computer Associates Micro
   Products
Computone Systems, Inc.
Compu-Shack Electronic
   GmbH
Comtrol Corporation
Conner Peripherals, Inc.
Control Systems, Inc.
Cordata Technologies, Inc.
Corollary, Inc.
CSS Laboratories, Inc.
Datamedia Corporation
Datatronic
Digital Communication
   Associates, Inc.
Digital Equipment Corp.
Digital Research, Inc.
Donatec Company
DPT
DTK Computer, Inc.
Epson America, Inc.
Everex Systems, Inc.
Excelan, Inc.
Future Domain Corporation
Hauppauge Computer Works
Headland Technology Inc.
Hewlett-Packard Company
HMC Technology Ltd.
IMC Networks
Information Builders, Inc.
Infotronic S.P.A.
Intel Corporation
Interactive Systems Corp.
Interphase Corporation
IOMEGA
Itausa Informatica S/A

ITT Cannon
I-Bus
Kaypro Corporation
Kayser Threde GmbH
Kontron Electroniks
Laguna Systems
Laser Computer, Inc.
Leukhardt Systems
Lotus Development
Lucid, Inc.
Madge Networks Ltd.
Matrox Electronic System
Medidata Informatica S/A
Methode Electronics, Inc.
Micro Computer Systems, Inc.
Micronics, Inc.
Micronyx, Inc.
Microsoft Corp.
Miniscribe
Mitac
Molex, Inc.
National Instruments
National Semiconductor Corp.
**NEC Information Systems,
   Inc.**
Nixdorf Computer AG
Nixdorf Computer Corp.
Nokia
Novell, Inc.
Oak Technologies, Inc.
Olivetti
Oracle Corporation
Parallax Computer Corp.
PC Calc Ltd.
Peter Norton Computing
Phoenix Technologies
Procomp USA, Inc.
Proteon, Inc.
Quantam Corporation

Quarterdeck Office Systems
QUME Corporation
Racal Interlan
Racore Computer Products
RC International
Renaissance-GRX, Inc.
Samsung
Santa Cruz Operation, Inc.
Scopus Technologia S/A
SMT Goupil
Souriau
Southwest Microsystems Inc.
Standard Microsystems Corp.
Star Gate Technology
Symantec Corporation
Symbolics, Inc.
Sytron Corp.
Tandon Corporation
Tandy
Tatung International
Tecmar, Inc.
Televideo Systems, Inc.

Texas Instruments
The Software Link
Thomas-Conrad Corp.
Tidewater Associates, Inc.
TMC Research Corporation
Torus Systems, Ltd.
Trident Computer, Inc.
Truevision, Inc.
Tulip Computer Intl. B.V.
Twinhead Corporation
Unisys Corporation
VIA Technologies
VLSI Technology, Inc.
Wang Laboratories
Wells America Corp.
WIPRO Information
    Technology, Ltd.
Wyse Technology
Zenith Data Systems Corp.
Zeos International
Zymos Marketing & Sales

Summary

As is obvious by the number and caliber of members, the EISA specification consortium is a powerful and committed force. Although their history is unusual in the level of cooperation that has been shown among otherwise competing companies, they have all made a commitment to the success of EISA, and with the computers announced so far from companies such as Hewlett-Packard and Compaq, that success appears assured.

Inside the EISA Computer

This chapter discusses the architecture of the EISA computer: the relationship of the CPU, RAM memory, ROM memory, I/O, and related concepts. It also discusses the function of the BIOS and how it relates to the computer hardware and the software such as the operating system and applications programs.

Figure 2-1 shows the structure of a typical computer in very general form. Note that it consists of only three parts: the CPU, the memory, and the I/O. The CPU, or Central Processing Unit, provides the "brains" of the computer. This may be an Intel 80486, a Motorola 68020, or one of many dozens of other processors. The memory stores programs and data while the computer is operating. When the power is turned off, most of the contents of this memory is lost. The I/O, or Input/Output functions, includes everything from the video display and keyboard interface to the operation of hard and floppy disk drives and the external ports for connecting printers, modems, and so forth.

The following paragraphs look at each of these areas in more depth. Although this discussion is geared towards the EISA com-

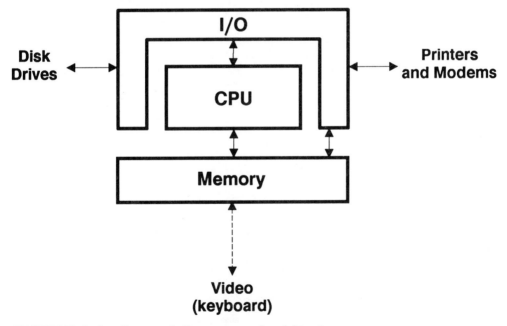

FIGURE 2-1   General Computer Architecture

puter, it applies equally to any of the PCs based on the Intel 8086, 80286, 80386, 80486, among others.

Central Processing Unit

The CPU consists of a number of registers (places that store and manipulate data) and a lot of logic circuitry to control what happens and when. Figure 2-2 shows a simplified functional block diagram of a CPU. In this case the CPU has 16 data lines and 32 address lines coming out of it. This means that it can read or write two bytes (2 × 8 bits) of data at a time and address 2^{32} memory addresses. A number of control lines also come out that control what the address and data lines do and when they do it.

Before going any further, a little detour into the world of computer numbering schemes is in order. Computers are binary devices, which means that all numbers are represented by binary numbers. In order to understand many aspects of computer operation, you need to understand the binary and hexadecimal numbering systems.

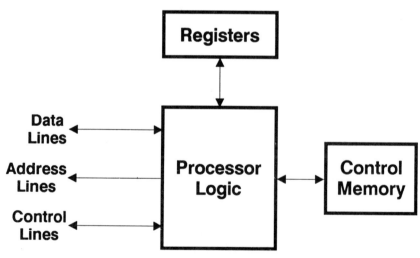

FIGURE 2-2   General CPU Architecture

The Binary Numbering System

Binary numbers are represented by 1s and 0s. For example, a 0 in binary is a 0 in decimal numbers. A 1 in binary is a 1 in decimal numbers. But there the similarity ends. A decimal 2 is too big to be represented by either a 0 or a 1, so we need a second digit. Figure 2-3 shows the decimal-binary relationship for some small numbers. For example, a decimal 2 is written in binary as 10. This means there is one unit of 2 and no unit of 1. An examination of Figure

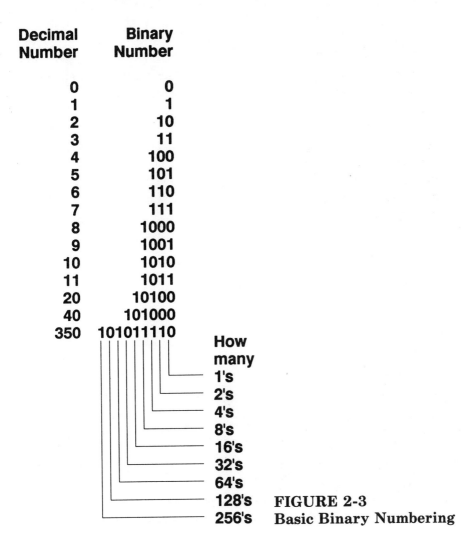

Decimal Number	Binary Number
0	0
1	1
2	10
3	11
4	100
5	101
6	110
7	111
8	1000
9	1001
10	1010
11	1011
20	10100
40	101000
350	101011110

How
many
1's
2's
4's
8's
16's
32's
64's
128's
256's

FIGURE 2-3
Basic Binary Numbering

2-3 shows how the binary numbering system expands to cover larger numbers.

Longer binary strings represent larger numbers. For example, Figure 2-4 shows an assortment of numbers that can be represented by 8 bits. As shown, 8 binary bits can represent decimal numbers from 0 to 255. Adding more bits increases the size of number that can be represented. Figure 2-4 also adds the leading 0s that are used in typical computer binary notation, thus showing a full byte.

The Hex Numbering System

Computers normally use a numbering system that is neither binary nor decimal. It is the hexadecimal numbering system, or hex, rep-

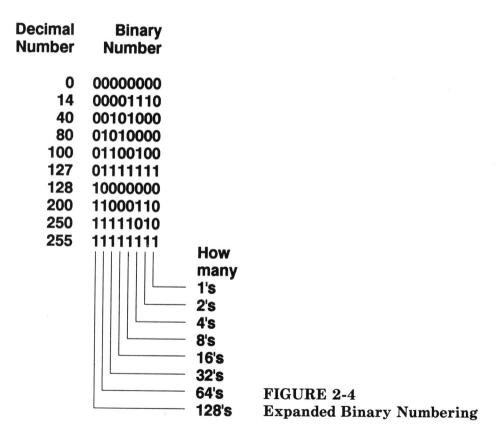

Decimal Number	Binary Number
0	00000000
14	00001110
40	00101000
80	01010000
100	01100100
127	01111111
128	10000000
200	11000110
250	11111010
255	11111111

How many
1's
2's
4's
8's
16's
32's
64's
128's

FIGURE 2-4
Expanded Binary Numbering

resented by the digits 0–9 and the letters A–F. Figure 2-5 shows the decimal and hex numbering systems with equivalents from 0 to 15 (0 to F hex) and some larger numbers that require two hex digits. Note that if you compare the hex numbers with their binary

Decimal Numbers	Hex Numbers	Binary Numbers
0	0	00000000
1	1	00000001
2	2	00000010
3	3	00000011
4	4	00000100
5	5	00000101
6	6	00000110
7	7	00000111
8	8	00001000
9	9	00001001
10	A	00001010
11	B	00001011
12	C	00001100
13	D	00001101
14	E	00001110
15	F	00001111
16	10	00010000
17	11	00010001
20	14	00010100
40	28	00101000
80	50	01010000
100	64	01100100
127	7F	01111111
128	80	10000000
200	C6	11001000
250	8A	11111010
255	FF	11111111
350	100	101011110

FIGURE 2-5   Basic Hex Numbering

equivalents, the larger digits are simply four binary digits per hex digit.

As with the binary and decimal numbering systems, larger numbers are represented with more digits. In EISA computers, data, addresses, and I/O locations are usually represented with the hex numbering system. It is common to encounter addresses like 0C32FBh, which equals 799483 decimal, or 11000011001011111011 binary.

Back to the CPU

This detour into numbering is relevant since the CPU's addresses and data are all represented in the hex numbering system. You first need to master this system if you are planning to learn or understand the concepts of programming.

Next, you will need to understand the operating concepts behind the CPU. They are best understood by tracing the operation of a typical CPU when the power is first applied.

Once the power is applied to all the electronics, a reset signal is sent to the CPU. This reset signal is generated by an external source, either a digital pulse generator or some type of RC network. (An RC network is a resistor/capacitor network that causes a time delay.)

The CPU responds to the reset signal by clearing out all its registers and setting the address lines to a specific address. In the case of the 80486, this address is FFFFFFF0h. (Here's where the hex numbering system is used. If you convert this to a binary number, you'll find that since each F equals 4 bits, the address bus contains 28 bits set to 1 and the last 4 set to 0.)

With the address lines set to a specific address, the CPU then reads the data lines to read in the data at that address. The typical EISA computer will have the first part of a boot routine at that address. As it reads the instruction at address FFFFFFF0h and up, it is instructed to jump to another address in the ROM. The program that the computer needs to run in order to start will be at this new address. These routines usually set up the serial and parallel ports, test the memory, and determine the hardware configuration of the system.

At this point, the CPU is instructed to read in the operating system software from a disk drive. Typically this will be from a hard drive, though the computer first checks to see if the floppy drive (usually drive A) contains a disk; if so, it boots from the floppy drive instead of the hard drive. This allows the user to boot a different version of the operating system than that which is on the hard disk, or to boot special operating systems or programs that contain their own operating systems. The EISA computers themselves are a good example, since many of them will boot up from a floppy disk during the initial setup procedure or at certain times when reconfiguring the system.

Once the system has booted up, the operating system, along with the programs and overlays called in by the CONFIG.SYS and AUTOEXEC.BAT files, determines the final configuration of the system. Let's now look at some of the other hardware aspects of an EISA computer system.

RAM and ROM

RAM (Random Access Memory) is the main memory of the computer. As programs are run, they first load into RAM from the disk drive, and the operating system then "jumps" to the beginning of the program to begin executing the program. Program data, such as the data in a spreadsheet or the text of a word processor, also loads into the computer's RAM. As changes are made in the data, the contents of the RAM are altered, and when the user finishes with the application, the revised data is copied back to the disk drive.

ROM (Read Only Memory) is the part of memory where, normally, the BIOS of the computer resides. The BIOS is the interface between the computer's hardware and the operating system and applications software. ROM is a "read only" device; you can read program information from it but you cannot write to it under most circumstances.

The size of the RAM and ROM, and the locations of various components, is shown with a memory map. This is a table (or graphic) representation of the memory locations. Table 2-1 shows a memory map of a typical EISA computer system.

TABLE 2-1   EISA Computer System Memory Map

Address	Description
00000000-0009FFFF	This area is the main system memory, and consists of 640K of RAM. Some systems may have only 512K, in which case their upper address will be 0008FFFF instead of 0009FFFF.
000A0000-000BFFFF	This 128K memory area is reserved for use by the video card.
000C0000-000DFFFF	This 128K memory area is reserved for additional ROMs normally used to expand the system's BIOS ROMs. This is usually a ROM on an EGA card.
000E0000-000FFFFF	This 128K memory area is reserved for option and BIOS ROMs.
00100000-03FFFFFF	This area is the rest of addressable memory up to 64MB. Some systems have the ability to address only 32MB of RAM and will end at address 01FFFFFF.

The remainder of the system's memory map is dependent on the particular requirements of the individual manufacturers.

I/O

I/O (Input/Output) is a mapped area similar to the memory map. Different addresses, or groups of addresses, are assigned to specific functions. However, the I/O map is much more extensive and complex, with different functions assigned to each of the addresses through 04FFh (1,280 addresses). If you need detailed information on the I/O map, you should obtain a copy of the EISA specification that details this information. A word of warning—this is technical engineering material and not casual reading for most people. Table 2-2 shows a summary of the I/O addresses.

TABLE 2-2   EISA Computer System I/O Map Summary

Address	Description
0000-00FF	ISA main system board components.
0100-03FF	ISA expansion cards.
0400-04FF	Reserved for main system board controllers.
0800-08FF	Reserved for the system board.
0C00-0CFF	Reserved for the system board.
1000-1FFF	Dedicated to expansion slot 1.
2000-2FFF	Dedicated to expansion slot 2.
3000-3FFF	Dedicated to expansion slot 3.
4000-4FFF	Dedicated to expansion slot 4.
5000-5FFF	Dedicated to expansion slot 5.
6000-6FFF	Dedicated to expansion slot 6.
7000-7FFF	Dedicated to expansion slot 7.
8000-8FFF	Dedicated to expansion slot 8.
9000-FFFF	Continuation of the address range from 1000-8FFF for additional expansion slots. Most EISA computers will have 8 slots.

EISA Computer Hardware

The EISA computers now coming on the market and those yet to be developed will come in a large variety of configurations. Models currently in development by a number of companies will sit on the desktop or at the deskside (on the floor). Both of these configurations offer nothing radically new in their packaging other than enhancements that the individual manufacturers may offer, such as the convenient front-panel power switches of the Hewlett-Packard versions. And in the not-too-distant future, it is possible that there will be portable models with an EISA slot or slots that will accommodate all of the new EISA boards soon to be announced.

The big difference between the current ISA computers and the new EISA computers will be the inside of the computers. They will contain a full complement of EISA connectors, and quite probably an Intel 80486 processor. Although the EISA bus is not restricted to a specific CPU, manufacturers are sure to continue to develop computers to the latest Intel CPU. One of the strengths of the EISA bus is its flexibility; it will be able to handle the processors of the future, in addition to the processors of today.

In fact, the only significant change will be the bus connector. Remember, one of the important advantages of the EISA bus it its ability to accommodate any of the over 1,000 cards currently available as well as cards yet to be developed.

The EISA Connector

The connector is truly innovative: it is fully compatible with all of the old cards and is designed to absolutely prevent damage if an old card is plugged into the EISA bus connector. Figure 2-6 shows a cutaway section of the new style of connector and how the connector fingers are staggered.

When an EISA card is plugged into the connector, the card goes past the top row of contacts and into the lower row. As the lower row of contacts on the EISA card goes past the upper contacts

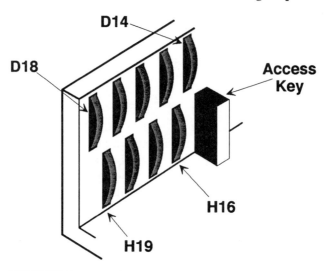

FIGURE 2-6   EISA Connector Finger Locations

in the connector, contact is not made since the connector contacts are centered between the connector fingers on the EISA card. As the card is pushed further into the connector, the lower row of contacts makes contact with the lower row of fingers on the card. At the same time, the upper row of contacts makes contact with the upper row of fingers on the card.

Insertion force, the difficulty of pushing the card into the connector, is not increased as a result of the additional number of contacts because most of the insertion force comes from pushing the connector contacts aside as the card is inserted, as shown in Figure 2-7. Once the contacts have been moved away to allow the board to slide in, the friction of the fingers is nominal. In fact, testing has shown that the insertion force is virtually the same for standard ISA connectors as it is for the standard EISA connector.

An ISA card cannot be pushed all the way into an EISA connector. As an ISA card is pushed into an EISA connector, small access keys prevent the card from being pushed further into the connector than is necessary, as shown in Figure 2-8. EISA cards can be pushed all the way in since the card is notched to allow it to get past the access keys, as shown in Figure 2-9.

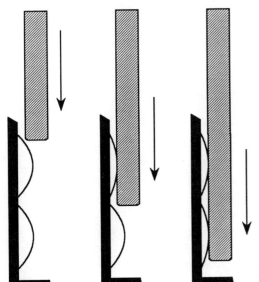

FIGURE 2-7
EISA Connector Finger Contacts

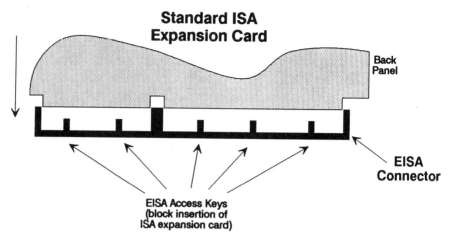

FIGURE 2-8   EISA Connector ISA Card Blocks

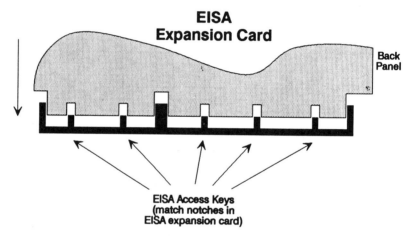

FIGURE 2-9   EISA Board Connector Notching

Figure 2-10 shows the signals appearing on the connector for an ISA card as dark pins that make up the upper row of connections on the connector. Note that the upper row of connector fingers is numbered exactly the same as the old ISA standard. Figure 2-11 shows the signals appearing on the connector for an EISA card as dark pins that make up the lower row of connections on the connector. Chapter 4, *The EISA Bus*, contains a complete discussion of the signals on the connector.

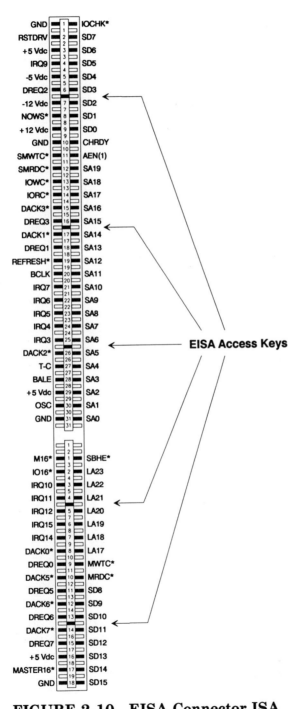

FIGURE 2-10   EISA Connector ISA Pins

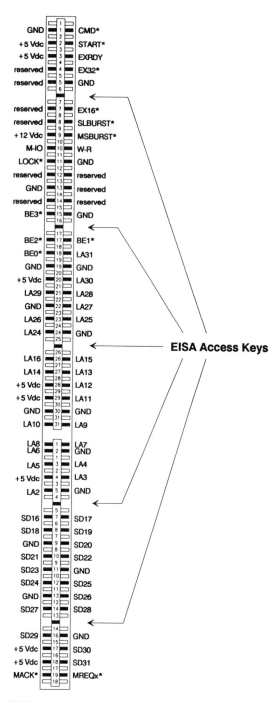

GND	CMD*
+5 Vdc	START*
+5 Vdc	EXRDY
reserved	EX32*
reserved	GND
reserved	EX16*
reserved	SLBURST*
+12 Vdc	MSBURST*
M-IO	W-R
LOCK*	GND
reserved	reserved
GND	reserved
reserved	reserved
BE3*	GND
BE2*	BE1*
BE0*	LA31
GND	GND
+5 Vdc	LA30
LA29	LA28
GND	LA27
LA26	LA25
LA24	GND
LA16	LA15
LA14	LA13
+5 Vdc	LA12
+5 Vdc	LA11
GND	GND
LA10	LA9
LA8	LA7
LA6	GND
LA5	LA4
+5 Vdc	LA3
LA2	GND
SD16	SD17
SD18	SD19
GND	SD20
SD21	SD22
SD23	GND
SD24	SD25
GND	SD26
SD27	SD28
SD29	GND
+5 Vdc	SD30
+5 Vdc	SD31
MACK*	MREQx*

EISA Access Keys

**FIGURE 2-11   EISA Connector
EISA Pins**

Beyond the new connectors there are few surprises in the new EISA computers. For example, some of the EISA computers will have the video circuitry, such as an EGA or VGA interface, built into the computer and others will have the video circuitry on a plug-in card. Some of the EISA computers will have one or two serial ports and one or two parallel ports built into the computer.

Card Size

Due to the freedom of defining a new standard, the EISA standard allows some fairly large cards to be plugged into the system. As shown in Figure 2-12, the area available for mounting components on the card measures 4.50 by 13.21 inches, which makes over 59 square inches of board area that can contain components. In addition, because of the advances made in a technology called SMT, or surface-mount technology (as opposed to the conventional method called through-hole mounting), components can now be mounted on both sides of the card. The EISA specification allows 0.525 inches on one side of the board (the side where components are normally mounted) and 0.150 inches on what is now called the solder side of the board. This 0.150 allows room for most of the surface-mount components, such as integrated circuits, capacitors,

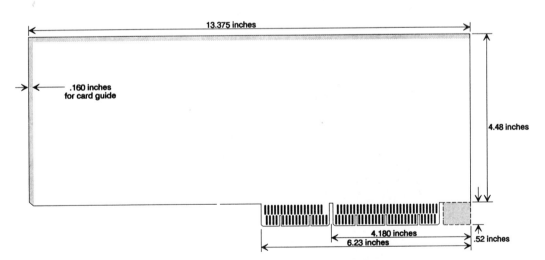

FIGURE 2-12   EISA Expansion Card Dimensions

and resistors, to be mounted. This yields a total usable board area of almost 120 square inches in a single card.

The EISA Component Interface

So far we've looked only at the architecture of a typical computer and at the EISA card and connector. The EISA hardware interface, a set of chips designed by Intel for the EISA computer bus, ties these together. This interface is called the 82350 EISA Chip Set and consists of an 82358 EISA Bus Controller, an 82357 Integrated System Peripheral, an 82352 EISA Bus Buffer, and an 82355 Bus Master Interface Controller. Figure 2-13 shows a functional block diagram of a typical EISA computer using the Intel 82350 chip set.

As shown in Figure 2-13, the CPU of most of the EISA computers will be either an 80386 or 80486. If the 80386 processor is used, a socket will normally be provided for the addition of a coprocessor such as the 80387. If an 80486 processor is used, the

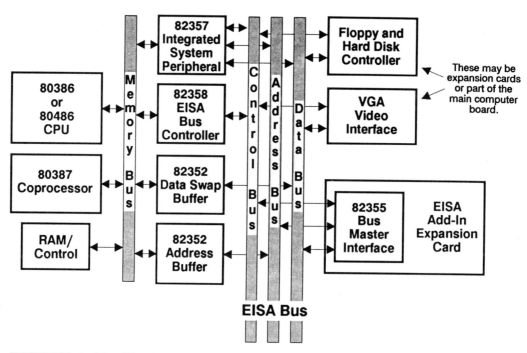

FIGURE 2-13   Typical EISA Computer Simplified Block Diagram

coprocessor socket is not required since the coprocessor is built into the processor. The functionality of each of the Intel chips is covered in more detail in the following sections.

82358 EISA Bus Controller

The EISA bus controller is the main component of all EISA systems. It provides an interface between the CPU and the EISA bus and an interface among the different buses of the EISA system. It provides translations among the cycles of the CPU, the ISA cards, the EISA cards, and generates ISA signals where necessary for the EISA bus masters. It provides an interface among multiple bus masters, and provides the timing functions that allow communications among the different buses. It provides EISA/ISA bus cycle compatibility in the EISA/ISA standard memory or I/O cycle, the EISA/ISA no wait-state cycle, the EISA compressed cycle, and the EISA burst cycles. It also provides control signals for the address buffers.

82357 Integrated System Peripheral

The integrated system peripheral chip works with the EISA bus controller to provide the system functions required in EISA applications. Most of these functions are similar to existing functions provided by a large number of components on existing systems, plus the addition of EISA-specific functions. These functions include a 7-channel DMA controller with full timing control for 8-, 16-, and 32-bit DMA transfers with up to 33MB per second data transfer rate, a bus arbitrator for bus sharing among multiple masters, a 15-level interrupt controller with the functionality of two 8259 controllers, refresh address generation and control functions, and five 16-bit counter/timers (8254 compatible) for interrupts and bus time-outs, DMA refresh requests, and other timing requirements.

82352 EISA Bus Buffer

The EISA bus buffer operates in three modes for use as data swap buffer logic, address buffers, and data parity buffers. It combines the functions typically provided by up to 17 separate components in previous designs, reducing the chip count, board complexity, and design complexity. By reducing the chip count, radio frequency interference generated by computer signals is reduced.

82355 Bus Master Interface Controller

The bus master interface controller is often located on each of the EISA add-in cards. It provides an interface among the functions of the add-in card and the address, data, and control lines of the EISA bus. It includes full support of burst mode for data transfer rates up to 33MB per second, and a 32-bit address bus which allows addressing 4GB as provided in the EISA specification. It also supports the EISA automatic configuration functions. There are two data transfer channels, which allows the processor to set up one data transfer while another is currently being performed.

Summary

The basic architecture of the EISA computers differs little from the ISA computers that have gained acceptance and familiarity over the past decade. The improvements are in the EISA bus connector, the new EISA chip set, and the software that is discussed in later chapters.

CHAPTER
3

The Operating System

This chapter covers the operating system of a typical EISA computer. Although there are a number of operating systems that will no doubt be used, among them DOS 3.3, OS/2, and UNIX, DOS 4 will be by far the most common. DOS 4 has the advantage of requiring less memory than operating systems such as OS/2 or UNIX, and it costs significantly less than either. Users requiring multitasking capability are likely to turn to additional programs such as Quarterdeck's Desqview or Microsoft's Windows running under DOS 4. Both provide excellent solutions to multitasking requirements, and each is best suited to specific applications.

In order to understand the operation and concepts of the operating system, we first need to look at the organization and structure of all the different types of software in the system.

Software Architecture

There are two structures in a personal computer, the software structure and the hardware structure. Chapter 2, *Inside the Computer*, discusses the hardware aspects of the computer and this chapter discusses the software structure.

Figure 3-1 shows the general relationship of the three functional areas of software in the computer. You are probably most familiar with the application programs. These are the programs you use to perform work on the computer, and might be anything from a word processing program, a database program, a spreadsheet program, a drawing or graphics program, to a game. These programs are the only kind that most computer users ever know or care about. An application program interface consists of its information on the screen and the keystrokes and mouse movements required to use the program. However, two other levels of software are also being run, and they are very important.

The next level down from the application program is the operating system (in this case, DOS). DOS accepts the commands from the keyboard or from the application software and causes things to happen, such as saving a file on disk or displaying the information on the screen. The third level is the BIOS (Basic Input/Output System). This software contains the hardware-specific instructions that tell DOS how to perform the requested task.

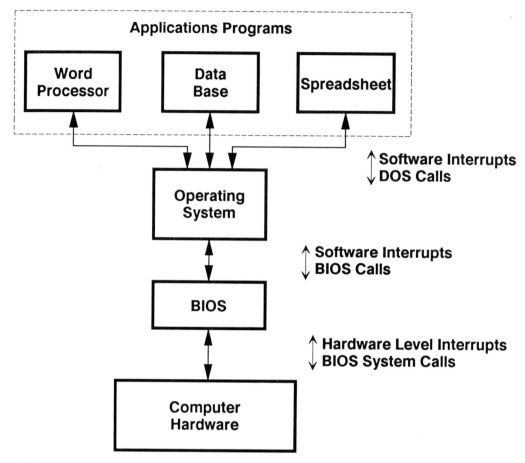

FIGURE 3-1   Software Structure

Communication among the various software entities takes place through program structures called "calls" and "interrupts." Figure 3-1 shows the communications paths among the various software system entities.

Each of the pieces shown in Figure 3-1 is seen in more detail in Figure 3-2.

BIOS

The BIOS software (often called firmware since it is not normally accessible or alterable) resides in a ROM (Read Only Memory).

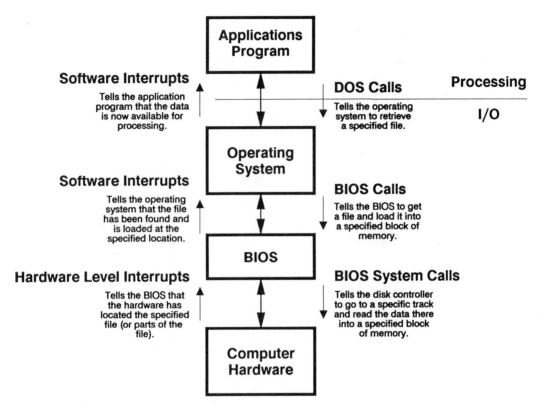

FIGURE 3-2   Software Structure Interface

The function of the BIOS is to provide an interface between the hardware and the software. In a sense, it translates the software commands and requirements into hardware commands. The BIOS is provided by the computer manufacturer and contains information that is particular to the specific hardware. In addition to this ROM BIOS, additional cards that plug into the computer may include BIOS extensions (additional software pertaining to those specific cards). Usually these would be cards such as a hard disk controller or an EGA card.

Using the example of a parallel printer output port, we will look at this in more detail. The component that interfaces the computer processor to the outside world has eight data lines that are connected to the data bus of the computer. In addition, there are other lines connected to the address lines and some of the control lines. When the control lines and address lines (under control of the microprocessor) tell the parallel interface to send a character out to the printer, the parallel interface looks at the data bus, gets the data, and sends it out to the printer. The instructions that tell the parallel interface to do this are contained in the ROM BIOS. Typically, these instructions are received from the operating system through BIOS calls. After completing the task, the BIOS responds through a software interrupt. An example of this technique is given in Chapter 9, *The Parallel Interface.*

The computer hardware accesses the BIOS through a scheme called hardware interrupts. When a signal comes in through one of the hardware interfaces (for example from the keyboard, a serial port, or a parallel port), it causes one of the hardware signal lines to change state. This change in state is called a hardware interrupt, and the system microprocessor responds to this interrupt as follows:

1. The interrupt causes the system microprocessor to pause and determine where the interrupt is coming from.

2. The system microprocessor then, through what is referred to as a system call, determines what the hardware wants. Usually, the hardware has a byte of information and wants the system microprocessor to accept it and do something with it, such as place it in memory.

3. The system microprocessor reads the byte of data, and sends it wherever it should go. The system microprocessor then returns to the previous task in progress before the interrupt occurred.

The ROM BIOS also provides a number of functions other than hardware interface and definition. When the computer is initially turned on (or reset), the CPU goes to the BIOS for operating instructions. The BIOS first verifies the proper operation of the system. This process, called a power-on test, provides a quick test of the computer's memory. Depending on the extent of the test and the amount of memory in the system, this process can take up to several minutes, though the typical test takes about 10 seconds. After the RAM is tested, the BIOS verifies a part of memory called

CMOS RAM. This is a special block of memory where the system configuration is stored. CMOS RAM is normally kept "alive" with a battery in the computer and is not lost when power is removed from the computer. Next, the BIOS determines what equipment is in the system. This information is contained in the CMOS RAM, and includes small programs which may need to be run to initialize some of the accessory cards plugged into the system.

After the testing and initializing is complete, the BIOS attempts to load the operating system from one of the disk drives. Normally, this is from a hard disk assigned as drive C, though it can be from any other hard disk or even from a floppy disk. Once the operating system is loaded in, the BIOS "jumps" to the operating system and the DOS prompt appears on the screen. The system is now ready to run programs.

Operating System

The middle level of software is the operating system, in this example MS-DOS 4.0, also called DOS. One of the functions of DOS is to provide a basic level of commands that allow the user to:

- examine information, such as displaying the directory of a disk (DIR)
- request file management functions, such as erasing some of the files (ERASE or DEL), or copying a file from one location (drive or subdirectory) to another (COPY).

The operating system also provides a standard software interface that can be accessed by application software.

The interface between DOS and the BIOS is handled through a standard set of software interrupts and BIOS calls. When the operating system wants a function performed, such as writing a file to disk, it first loads certain registers with information about the file, such as where it is and how big it is. It then jumps to a routine in the BIOS to read the registers and write the file to disk.

Application Software

Application software is the final level in the software structure. It includes applications like word processing and spreadsheet programs, as well as utilities such as the configuration program that all EISA computers use to initially set up the computer and later make changes to the system configuration. In addition to these programs, a large number of utility programs are provided with DOS and from other sources. These utility programs do things like display the directory in different formats, back up the hard disk, or alter display characteristics.

Virtually all of the processing takes place through application software. For every instruction sent to the operating system or BIOS, hundreds are used within the application program to calculate what should be done. For example, if you are running a spreadsheet program and the program recalculates some of the cells, it is the spreadsheet program that is doing all the work. The only time the processor goes out to the operating system (or sometimes directly to the BIOS) is when it is actually updating the video screen.

DOS 4 Overview

This section describes the DOS 4 operating system in greater detail.

DOS 4 is similar to DOS 3.3 in many areas, enough so that a person familiar with DOS 3.3 will not need to learn anything new to be both comfortable and productive. However, DOS 4 does add some nice features. For example:

- Hard disks greater than 32MB are supported without partitioning. For example, this means that you can have a hard disk of 150MB partitioned as drive C with 30MB and drive D with 120MB. Also, because of the expansion of the 16-bit logical sector numbers to 32-bit size, DOS 4 can handle disk sizes of up to 2GB (2000MB).

- DOS 4 provides an optional shell program that operates in a menu style. For many users, the DOS command line is difficult to use, and they prefer an icon or menu type user interface. Now users have a choice between a menu, a command line, or both.

- The Expanded Memory Specification (EMS) written to the Lotus/Intel/Microsoft (LIM 4.0) standard is fully supported by DOS 4. This means the computer will easily handle much more memory, (depending on the implementation, from 4MB to 64MB of additional memory). The INT 67H interface, defined by the LIM 4.0 specification, provides access to the memory. This maximizes compatibility with existing products designed for compatibility with LIM 4.0 specification. The LIM 4.0 emulator is provided with the file *memm.sys*.

- Installation of the DOS 4.0 operating system is performed through a menu-style interface, the **select** program, making installation easier for the novice user.

- The video support has been improved to allow the printing of graphics screens and displaying more lines of text.

- Many of the programs (commands) that come with DOS have been enhanced.

DOS 4 File Structures

Files, and the way they are stored on disk, are often compared to a row of filing cabinets containing a number of drawers, each drawer containing a number of folders, and each folder containing a number of documents. Although this comparison can be confusing, it effectively shows how DOS starts with a single undivided storage area (the root directory), and expands by adding subdirectories. Figure 3-3 shows the organization of a possible system.

The files begin at the left with the root directory. This is usually the point where all the directories are located and, typically, very few files are stored here.

Usually, each of the directories is dedicated to a particular function, such as all the EISA files, or word processing, or a spreadsheet, or games. Going into the directory for games, for example, you might find chess, checkers, and poker. In fact, the games directory could contain subdirectories that contain different versions of chess games or poker games.

DOS 4 Enhancements

DOS is an evolutionary operating system. It has come from its original version (nominally 1.0) to its present version of 4.01. There

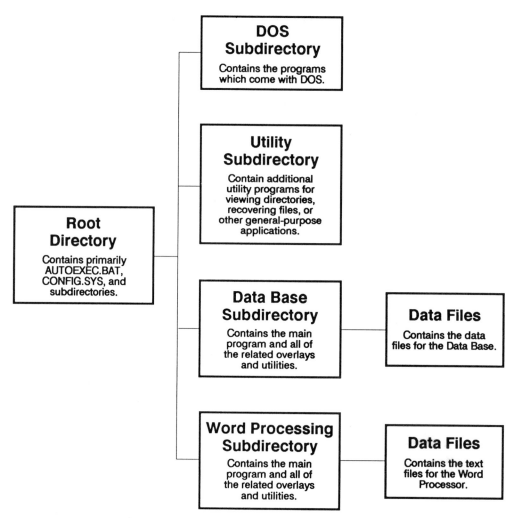

FIGURE 3-3   File Organization

will, no doubt, be another version of DOS to succeed version 4, probably version 5. There are also variations on the theme, such as Presentation Manager, OS/2, and Windows. However, this book will concern itself with DOS version 4 and comparison with its popular predecessor, DOS 3.3. The following sections discuss the benefits of the new version of DOS, and discuss in general terms the command set of DOS 4. A complete discussion of DOS 4 is beyond the scope of this book, and I recommend you obtain a copy of *Expert Advisor: DOS* by Jonathan Kamin (Addison-Wesley, 1989). However, a summary of the commands is presented here along with the enhancements in DOS 4.

The **select** command provides an enhanced installation program that makes installation and system configuration simple. It also creates the required *config.sys* and *autoexec.bat* files. Using **select**, the user can install DOS 4 either on an existing system using an earlier version of DOS, or on a new system with an empty formatted disk.

The **mem** command is new and provides complete information on the memory being used, how it is configured, and what programs are loaded.

The **tree** command is more graphical, making the structure of the disk easier to understand.

The **del** command can be told to display a prompt before it deletes a file.

Graphics support is provided for EGA and VGA displays, and the graphics support also includes a number of printers for screen dumps. Video support in DOS 4 covers everything from the original monochrome and CGA modes to the VGA modes. **cls**, **dir**, **more**, **edlin**, **con** and *ansi.sys* are now sensitive to the video mode and will display properly according to the current screen length. In addition, **graphics** has been extended to support the graphics modes for the EGA and VGA display.

A number of other commands have been enhanced to provide additional functions. Most of these enhancements provide compatibility with the new video displays and the larger hard disk formats.

Certain manufacturers, such as Hewlett-Packard and Compaq, have provided additional features that apply primarily to their own machines. These include features like disk caching (allows the computer to get to frequently accessed files faster) and more advanced and sophisticated memory management (allowing the use of RAM as a disk drive, or the use of larger amounts of memory, ranging from 1 to 64MB).

DOS 4 Commands and Programs

DOS 4 provides a number of commands that are used for manipulating files, data, and system configuration. These commands are

in two formats, programs that reside on the disk and are loaded
and executed every time they are used, and commands which are
a part of DOS and reside in the operating system when it is loaded
in memory. In the following descriptions the term "command" will
refer to memory resident (DOS) commands and the term "program" will refer to programs which, though a part of DOS, reside
on a disk and are loaded each time they are used.

This is not a complete description of the commands, but
rather a summary of the commands highlighting the elements that
are new for DOS 4. Refer to the documentation that came with
DOS 4 for a complete description of the commands.

append program	Allows the user to define the search path for data files. This is often used with word processing, database, and spreadsheet programs to tell programs where to search for data files, much like the **path** command defines where to look for executable files. Also see the **path** command for a similar function.
assign program	Reassigns the disk requests. For example, when a program has been told to look for files on drive C:, the **assign** command can make the computer look for the files on drive A: instead.
attrib program	Changes the status of the archive and read-only status bits for a file or group of files. This is often used with batch-type backup programs or when write-protecting or hiding files.

backup program

Allows the user to make a backup copy of files. Typically this command is used to back up files from a hard disk to floppy disks for archiving in the event of a hard disk failure. Also see the program **restore** for a complementary function. In the DOS 4 version of **backup**, the program will default to the /f switch mode (formats the destination floppy disk). Also, the DOS 4 version allows the user to place the *backup.log* file on the target drive.

break command

Makes Ctrl-Break and Ctrl-C operate at all times, rather than just during keyboard, video, and printer input/output operations.

cd or **chdir** command

Allows the user to move around between the different directories on a drive.

chkdsk program

Tests the condition of a disk or files on a disk. If any files, or the disk itself, are found to have a problem, it is reported. Note that this is not a complete disk check, though it provides a reliable check of the integrity of the files and directory on the disk.

comp program

Compares two files and displays the differences between the files. **comp** is normally only used to compare executable files and not data. Also see the **fc** program for a similar function.

copy command

Copies from one disk (source) to another (destination). Also see the program **xcopy** for a similar but more enhanced function.

ctty command

Allows the user to change the console from the normal keyboard and display to another I/O device. This is often used to allow the computer to be run from another location over a modem connected to one of the serial ports.

date command	Allows the user to display or change the date information in the computer. Also see the **time** command for a similar function.
debug program	Included with DOS 4 from most manufacturers. It is a debugging/programming tool normally used by programmers for testing new applications programs, though it can be used for many other jobs, such as patching programs or examining files for format. The DOS 4 version of **debug** has been enhanced to support expanded memory with four new commands, **XA**, **XD**, **XM** and **XS**.
del or **erase** command	Allows the user to delete files from a disk. On the DOS 4 version, there is a /p option which will allow the user to be prompted for deletion if the /p option is used.
dir command	Allows the user to display a listing of the files in a directory.
diskcomp program	Allows the user to compare two disks. This works only on floppy disks, not hard disks.
diskcopy program	Allows the user to copy one disk (source) to another (destination). This makes an exact copy of the source disk, and is not used for copying a partial disk or selected files.
edlin program	Included with DOS 4 from most manufacturers. It is a very fast line-oriented editor, adequate for most programming needs.
exe2bin program	Converts an executable file (.EXE) to a binary file (.COM). Binary format files are usually smaller and load faster.
exit command	Exits the DOS command processor. It is usually used to return the system to an alternative command processor or shell.

fastopen program

Reduces the time required to load frequently used files by keeping track of the files on the disk. DOS 4 added new functions to speed up directory search and data search operations. The /e option allows the cache to be located in LIM 4.0 expanded memory, allowing **buffers**= in the *config.sys* file to be increased to 10,000 (assuming the user has adequate RAM to support it).

fc program

Allows the user to compare the contents of two files. Usually, **fc** is used to compare only data files, not executable programs. Also see the **comp** program for a similar function.

fdisk program

Divides a hard disk into sections called partitions. These partitions then appear as separate disk drives, such as C:, D:, and E:. In DOS 4, this program has been enhanced to accept disk partitions in megabytes or percentages, and to display the volume label and file system type for each of the partitions.

find program

Examines files to find a specified string of characters in the file or files.

format program

Formats a disk so that it can store files. Typically, formatting is required before you can use floppy or hard disks. The DOS 4 version has been updated to require a volume label, and the /v switch is ignored.

graphics program

Allows the user to print a graphic screen on a compatible graphics printer. These printers include the entire HP "Jet" series of printers, as well as some IBM and other manufacturers. In the DOS 4 version, the EGA and VGA display adapters are fully supported, as are additional printers.

join program

Combines two physical disk drives into a single logical drive. The second physical drive usually becomes a directory on the logical drive.

keyb program

Allows the user to redefine the keyboard. This is usually done to accommodate the characters on foreign language keyboards.

label program

Changes the 11-character volume label on a disk. Also see the **vol** command.

md or **mkdir** command

Creates a new directory or subdirectory.

mem program

Displays information about the computer's memory status. This is a new program for DOS 4, and is fully compatible with the LIM 4.0 specification for displaying memory information.

mode program

Alters the configuration of DOS to accommodate altered system configurations. For example, it can redirect printer output from the parallel port to a serial port, or alter the settings of a serial port. **mode** also changes the display modes, the serial and parallel port modes, and the keyboard or code page-switching modes. DOS 4 added the ability to select typematic rates, additional number of lines per screen, new print parameters, and Async parameters.

more program

Pauses the screen after it has scrolled up a full page. This is often used with the **type** and **dir** commands.

nlsfunc program

Provides support for foreign language installations.

path command

Defines the path that DOS searches to find an executable program. Also see the **append** program for a similar function.

print program	Allows the user, from a print queue, to print files in the background while other programs are being run.
prompt command	Allows the user to change the DOS command prompt to a different character, and to display additional system information each time the command line is displayed.
rd or **rmdir** command	Allows the user to remove a directory or subdirectory from a disk. This is the opposite of the **md** or **mkdir** command.
recover program	Allows the user to recover a file which is written on a bad sector on a disk.
ren or **rename** command	Allows the user to rename a file.
replace command	Allows the user to replace files on a disk or add new files. Also see the **copy** command and the **xcopy** program.
restore program	Allows the user to restore files from a set of backup disks to a (typically) hard disk. Also see the **backup** program.
select program	Installs the DOS 4 operating system and configures it for your system. It is new to DOS 4.
set command	Used to define or alter the DOS environment.
share program	Used in a network environment to support file sharing functions.
sort program	Allows the user to sort data in a file.
subst program	Allows the user to substitute a virtual drive for a physical drive (and/or path).
sys program	Allows the user to install a copy of the operating system on a formatted disk.
time command	Allows the user to display or change the time information in the computer. Also see the **date** command for a similar function.

tree program	Allows the user to examine the directory structure of a disk drive. On the DOS 4 version, the tree display is indented at each directory level and block graphics are used to make the structure clearer.
type command	Allows the user to view the contents of a file on the screen. A change in the _command.com_ program allows the **type** command to display the entire contents of a file. In earlier versions, an **eof** character in the file would terminate the **type** command.
ver command	Allows the user to determine the version of DOS that you are running.
verify command	Allows the user to enable or disable the ability of DOS to verify the accuracy of information written to a disk.
vol command	Displays the volume label of the disk. Also see the **label** program.
xcopy program	Allows the user to copy files from one disk/directory to another, including subdirectories. This program is similar to the **copy** command.

Other File Types

Several other types of files should be mentioned here. The first is the _config.sys_ file, which DOS uses to load other **.sys** files into the computer's memory when power is first turned on. The second type is the batch file, of which there are two categories:

1. The _autoexec.bat_ file that the computer examines when power is first applied.

2. Other batch files, usually used to perform frequent though redundant tasks.

config.sys   The *config.sys* file provides a means of configuring your system to suit your particular needs. When the *config.sys* file is placed in the root directory (it is OK to "hide" the file using the **attrib** program), DOS will look for it every time the system is reset or powered-up. If DOS finds the *config.sys* file, it adjusts the configuration of DOS in accordance with the parameters specified in the *config.sys* file. The following pages provide a brief overview of the configuration commands. If you need detailed information, refer to the documentation that came with your version of DOS 4.

break command	Tells DOS to check for a Ctrl-Break or Ctrl-C at all times (**break**=on) or only during standard I/O (**break**=off).
buffers command	Tells DOS how many 528-byte disk buffers to allocate. With a conventional 640K memory system, the number of buffers is limited to 99. If you have an expanded memory, you can use the /x option and have whatever will fit into expanded memory, up to 10,000 buffers. Although adding disk buffers usually increases the speed of disk access, thus increasing the apparent speed of program execution, the tradeoff is that they use program memory, making programs which are memory intensive difficult, if not impossible, to run.
country command	Defines the display format for the country for which the user has configured DOS.
device command	Allows DOS to load additional device drivers into the operating system. Examples of these drivers are *ansi.sys* that allows use of ANSI escape sequences when addressing the screen, or *ramdrive.sys* that allows part of your memory to be used as a disk drive.

drivparm command	Allows the user to define disk drive parameters for additional disk drives. This is often used when installing a disk drive with unusual parameters, such as an unusual number of tracks or sectors.
fcbs command	Defines how many files can be open at once, using file control blocks. The default is 4, though application programs such as databases and word processing programs may require a larger number. If an increase in the number of files that can be open is required, this information should be provided by the publisher of the application software.
files command	Defines how many files can be open at once using handles. As with the **fcbs** command above, the default is 4, though application programs such as databases and word processing programs may require a larger number.
install command	Allows the user to execute four commands; **fastopen.exe, keyb.exe, nlsfunc.exe,** or **share.exe.**
lastdrive command	Allows the user to specify the last drive in his system. The default is 5 drives (E:), though the value can be set up to 26 to allow access to drive Z. This is often used on systems on a network such as the HP ThinLan where the system administrator may assign the network or networks, for example, as drives N:, O:, and P:.
rem command	Allows a command for comments, REM, to be inserted in the *config.sys* file. This is a new command for DOS 4.

shell command   Specifies the command processor from which the computer will start when the user first turns it on or does a system reset. These command processors, or shells, typically provide an easier-to-use interface into DOS, such as the Hewlett-Packard PAM program.

stacks command   Allows the user to redefine the number and size of the stack frames. Since DOS uses these stacks each time an interrupt occurs, an insufficient number of stack frames could cause the system to crash.

Autoexec.bat   The *autoexec.bat* file is typically located in the root directory and is executed every time the computer is powered up or reset. It usually contains the names of one or more programs that are executed before you begin to use the computer. These might be programs to set up a RAM disk drive and move files into the drive, or to put a clock display in the corner of the screen.

Batch Files   Another category of files is the batch file. These files can be created to abbreviate a sequence of keystrokes that you type when starting up an often-used program.

For example, if your word processing program starts up with the command line:

```
WORDPROC V 80 25 D
```

to start up the program WORDPROC in VGA display mode with 80 characters across and 25 lines down in document mode, you could simplify this with a batch file. Using your text editor, create a batch file with the following line in it:

```
WORDPROC V 80 25 D
```

Name the file *w.bat*. Now, every time you type **W** and press return, the operating system will find the batch file *w.bat* and input the contents of the batch file to the computer instead of your having to type it. The batch file is a rudimentary form of programming, for you have simply written a program to tell the computer to run WORDPROC V 80 25 D every time you type **W**. Of course, you have to make sure there is no program named *w.com* or *w.exe* on the computer, or you will have a conflict.

Batch files execute some commands as a set of programming instructions. These are listed and defined as follows:

call command — Allows the user to run one batch file from another. Otherwise one batch file must be ended before running another.

echo command — Allows the user to turn the video display screen off when running the batch file, so that the commands from the batch file are not displayed as the batch file runs the programs. This will not turn off messages displayed by the program itself.

for command — Runs a program or executes a command based on a test of values. This is similar to a **for** command in programming.

goto command — Allows the user to tell the batch file to jump to a specified location in the batch file and begin executing from that location. These locations are addressed with labels in the batch file.

if command — Allows the batch file to test for a condition and then branch if that condition meets a defined condition.

pause command — Temporarily halts the processing of the batch file and allows the batch file to display a message before continuing.

rem command — Allows the user to insert remark comments into the batch file, thus making troubleshooting or later changes easier.

shift command   Allows use of more than ten command line parameters in the batch file.

Summary

The EISA computers are designed to use both existing operating systems and future operating systems such as those based on OS/2, UNIX, and others. However, most of the EISA computers use the DOS 4.0 operating system. The structure of DOS 4.0 is basically the same as the existing systems of today's ISA computers, but with some enhancements to make it easier to use and more complete. Calls and interrupts are basically the same, and file structures are altered only to allow for the significantly larger hard drives that are being introduced with the EISA computers.

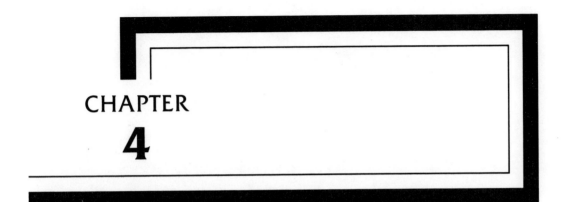

CHAPTER
4

The EISA Bus

This chapter discusses the electrical characteristics of the EISA bus connector. The function of each of the pins is summarized and identified as either an ISA or EISA pin.

The EISA connector consists of two rows of contacts. The upper row of pins provides connection to the original ISA board contact pins. The lower row of pins provides connection to the new EISA pins. As discussed in Chapter 2, *Inside the Computer*, the connector has five access keys to keep ISA cards from making contact with the EISA contacts.

Signal levels are fully compatible with those of the ISA specification, and are provided in detail in the Intel chip set documentation. Note that each of the signal lines may have different characteristics depending on the bus line's requirements, and conformance to the Intel specifications must be verified for proper circuit operation.

The pinouts of the entire EISA connector are shown in Figure 4-1. The inner rows of pins are the upper, or ISA, contacts. The outer rows of pins are the lower, or EISA, contacts.

The ISA pins duplicate the standard ISA bus in order to maintain compatibility with the earlier ISA cards. The EISA pins provide all the additional functionality of the new EISA bus, including expansion of the data bus to 32 bits and significantly improved DMA and interrupt handling. These are described in more detail in Chapter 5, *EISA Computer Interrupts, DMA, and I/O Structure*.

The function of each of the pins on the bus is described in the following pages. The descriptions are provided to give you a general understanding of the functionality of the EISA bus. If you need specific information, such as timing between the bus signals, you should refer to the EISA specification, containing over 200 pages of detailed bus functionality and timing information. In certain of the signal descriptions the term "bus master" is used. This applies equally to a card plugged into the EISA bus, or to the CPU on the main processor board (usually the motherboard).

Bus Differences

The differences between the EISA and the old ISA bus are the addition of 16 data lines, 23 address lines, and 16 additional in-

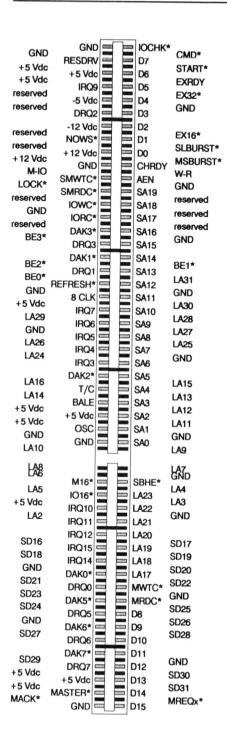

FIGURE 4-1
The EISA Bus Connector

dicator and control lines. A brief definition of each of the signal lines, both ISA and EISA, follows.

Address and Data Bus Signals

Signal	Signal Type	Definition
BE˜<3:0>	EISA	Provides a byte-enable function used to identify specific bytes as addressed in a dword (double word, or 4 bytes).
D<31:16>	EISA	Bits 31:24 are the highest 8 bits of a dword and are enabled when BE3˜ is asserted for 32-bit devices. Bits 23:16 are the second highest 8 bits of a dword and are enabled when BE2˜ is asserted for 32-bit devices.
D<15:0>	ISA	Bits 15:8 are the third highest 8 bits of a dword and are enabled when BE1˜ is asserted for 32-bit devices. Bits 7:0 are the lowest 8 bits of a dword and are enabled when BE0˜ is asserted for 32-bit devices.
LA<16:2>	EISA	Latchable address lines, part of the 32-bit latchable address bus.
LA<23:17>	ISA	Latchable address lines, part of the 32-bit latchable address bus; however, they are located in the ISA part of the connector.
LA<31:24>˜	EISA	Latchable address lines, part of the 32-bit latchable address bus. They are similar to LA<16:2> except their levels are inverted. That is, a **1** is an address bit of **0**, and a **0** is an address bit of **1**.

SA<19:0>	ISA	Addresses I/O or memory devices, forming the lowest 20 bits of the 32-bit address scheme.
SBHE~	ISA	Indicates that cards using 16-bit transfers should drive data on the D<15:8> lines of the data bus.
AENx	ISA	Slot-specific; used to enable cards in a specific slot for I/O and address commands.

Data Transfer Control Signals

Signal	Signal Type	Definition
BCLK	ISA	Synchronizes bus functions with the main system clock.
MSBURST~	EISA	Indicates to a slave that the bus master can provide burst cycles.
SLBURST~	EISA	Used by a bus slave to indicate that it supports burst cycles.
M-IO	EISA	Used by bus master to identify whether a memory (high) or I/O (low) cycle is in process.
LOCK~	EISA	Used by the bus master to mandate exclusive access to the memory during the time LOCK~ is asserted.
EX32~	EISA	Used by a slave to indicate that it supports 32-bit data transfers.
EX16~	EISA	Used by a slave to indicate that it supports 16-bit data transfers.
EXRDY	EISA	Used by a slave to request wait state timing.
START~	EISA	Provides timing control from the bus master to indicate the start of a cycle.

CMD~	EISA	Provides timing control of a command.
W-R	EISA	Differentiates between a write (high) or read (low) cycle.
BALE	ISA	Active when a valid address is available on the LA⟨31:2⟩ address lines.
MRDC~	ISA	Indicates that the memory slave should put its data on the memory bus.
MWTC~	ISA	Indicates that the data on the memory bus is valid and may be latched.
SMWTC~	ISA	Indicates that the data on the memory bus is valid and may be latched. This signal is derived from MWTC~.
SMRDC~	ISA	Indicates that the memory slave should put its data on the memory bus. This signal is derived from MRDC~.
IOWC~	ISA	Indicates that a DMA device can latch data from the data bus.
IORC~	ISA	Indicates that a DMA device can put data on the data bus.
CHRDY	ISA	Lengthens a bus cycle.
NOWS~	ISA	Indicates that the memory slave does not require the remaining clock cycles.
M16~	ISA	Indicates that the memory is capable of a 16-bit data transfer.
IO16~	ISA	Indicates that the I/O slave is capable of a 16-bit data transfer.

Bus Arbitration Signals

Signal	Signal Type	Definition
MREQx~	EISA	Slot specific; allows specific bus masters to request access to the bus.
MAKx~	EISA	Used by the system board to grant bus access when requested by the MREQx~ signal.
DRQ<7:5,3:0>	ISA	Request a DMA response from a subsystem, or allow an ISA bus master to request access to the bus.
DAK~<7:5,3:0>	ISA	Acknowledge that a DMA channel has been granted access to the bus.
T-C	ISA	In the output mode, indicates that a DMA channel has reached terminal word count. In the input mode, used to stop a DMA transfer.
MASTER16~	ISA	Indicates a 16-bit data size by the bus master.
REFRESH~	ISA	Indicates when a memory refresh cycle is in process.

Utility Signals

Signal	Signal Type	Definition
OSC	ISA	Provides a 14.31818 MHz, 50% duty cycle, clock signal.
RESDRV	ISA	Resets the cards in the expansion connectors.
IRQ<15,14,12:9,7:3>	ISA	Interrupt the CPU to request service.

| IOCHK~ | ISA | Tells the main CPU that an error has occurred. This normally results in a nonmaskable interrupt (NMI). |

Signal Use

The use of each of the signals (or signal groups) of the EISA bus is shown below. The signals are differentiated as to EISA or ISA, and whether they are used for Input, Output, or both (Input/Output). The function is referenced from the perspective of the system board.

EISA Signals

Signal	Input/Output
BE~<3:0>	I/O
CMD~	O
EX16~	I/O
EX32~	I/O
EXRDY	I/O
LA<31:2>	I/O
LOCK~	O
MAKx~	O
MREQx~	I
MSBURST~	I/O
M-IO	I/O
SLBURST~	I
START~	I/O
W-R	I/O

ISA Signals

Signal	Input/Output
AENx	O
BALE	O
BCLK	O
CHRDY	I/O
DAK~<7:5,3:0>	O
DRQ<7:5,3:0>	I
D<31:0>	I/O
IO16~	I
IOCHK~	I
IORC~	I/O
IOWC~	I/O
IRQ<15,14,12:9,7:3>	I
M16~	I/O
MASTER16~	I
MRDC~	I/O
MWTC~	I/O
NOWS~	I
OSC	O
REFRESH~	I/O
RESDRV	O
SA<19:0>	I/O
SBHE~	I/O
SMRDC~	O
SMWTC~	O
T-C	I/O

Connector Specifications

As you can see from the following specifications, the connector is quite rugged. The insertion force for installing cards, in spite of all the additional pins, is approximately the same as the ISA connector (28 lbs.).

Insertion force	28 lbs. through ISA contacts
	35 lbs. maximum ISA and EISA contacts
Durability	100 cycles minimum
Contact force	.167 lbs. minimum
Contact resistance	30 milliohms maximum (new)
	40 milliohms maximum (100 insertions)
Contact current	1 Amp per contact on EISA contacts
	3 Amps per contact on ISA contacts
Thermal	Contacts and housing will withstand all vapor phases and surface mount processes
Humidity	90-95% RH at 40 degrees Centigrade
Vibration	10 Gs, 10-500 Hz, 3 hours
Physical Shock	100 Gs, 6 ms sawtooth, 18 shocks
Housing	Glass-filled thermoplastic UL 94 V-O
Contact	Copper alloy
Contact plating	Gold flash in the contact area, tin lead on the solder tails.
Inter-contact capacitance	Less than 2 picofarads between adjacent contacts

Summary

An EISA bus slot accepts an ISA standard card and offers it complete ISA functionality. But beyond an ISA compatible connector, the full scope of EISA bus functionality is available in the same dual-use slot. Expansion of the data bus to 32 bits by combining the original 16-bit ISA bus with an additional 16 bits from the EISA bus, plus improved interrupt and DMA handling, makes the EISA bus a very powerful and logical next generation in personal computers.

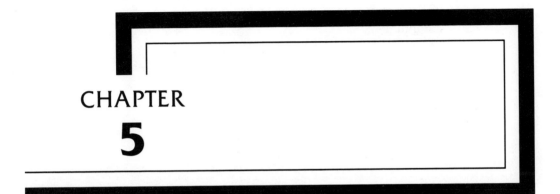

CHAPTER
5

The EISA
Interrupts, DMA,
and I/O Structures

The EISA computer systems, while compatible with the ISA computers, offer a number of enhancements that provide improved operation of interrupts and DMA.

The following pages present an overview of the interrupts, Direct Memory Access (DMA), and I/O information as provided in the EISA specification. If you need detailed information, consult the EISA specification. It provides complete information on all of the registers down to the bit level.

Interrupts

The EISA computer systems have an ISA-compatible interrupt controller. Interrupts can be either edge sensitive for ISA compatibility or level sensitive. Level triggered operation allows a single interrupt to be shared by more than one device, such as two serial ports.

The EISA interrupt controller provides 15 interrupts (0, 1, 3–15), with interrupt 2 used to cascade interrupts from the slave interrupt controller (interrupts 8–15) to the master controller (0–7). By cascading the slave interrupt controller into interrupt 2 of the master controller, the priority is as follows:

IRQ0

IRQ1

IRQ8

IRQ9

IRQ10

IRQ11

IRQ12

IRQ13

IRQ14

IRQ15

IRQ3

IRQ4

IRQ5

IRQ6

IRQ7

Interrupt Controller I/O Addresses

The interrupt controller is mapped to I/O addresses, as shown in Table 5-1.

TABLE 5-1   Interrupt Controller Address Map

Interrupt Block	I/O Address	Register Name
IRQ<7:0>	020h	INT-1 Base Address
IRQ<7:0>	021h	INT-1 Mask Register
IRQ<7:0>	4D0h	INT-1 Edge/Level Register
IRQ<15:8>	0A0h	INT-2 Base Address
IRQ<15:8>	0A1h	INT-2 Mask Register
IRQ<15:8>	4D1h	INT-2 Edge/Level Register

Interrupt Sequence

The interrupt sequence is summarized as follows:

1. One of the interrupt lines is asserted: that sets the corresponding bit in the Interrupt Request register.

2. The interrupt controller checks the request and interrupts the CPU.

3. The CPU responds with an interrupt acknowledge cycle.

4. The interrupt controller clears the interrupt request bit and sets the proper in-service register bit.

5. The CPU performs a second interrupt acknowledge cycle to read the interrupt vector on data lines D<7-0>. This consists of the interrupt code on bits D<2:0> and the vector address on bits D<7:3>.

This completes the interrupt cycle. Depending on the mode, the in-service register bit is cleared at the end of the second interrupt acknowledge or when an appropriate end-of-interrupt command is issued.

The initialization sequence for the interrupt controller is covered in the full EISA specification, and is beyond the scope of this book. The specification provides detailed information.

Non-Maskable Interrupts

Non-maskable interrupts indicate error conditions. The Non-Maskable Interrupt register is I/O mapped as shown in Table 5-2.

Full information on programming the NMI registers is available in the EISA specification.

TABLE 5-2   NMI Register Map

Register	I/O Address	R/W
NMI Status Register	061h	RW
NMI Enable Register	070h	W
Extended NMI Register	461h	RW
Software NMI Register	462h	W

Interval Timers

The EISA system provides interval timers that are compatible with the Intel 8254 Programmable Interval Timers as used in most ISA systems. Their functions are shown in Table 5-3.

TABLE 5-3   Interval Timer Functions

Timer	Counter	Function
1	0	IRQ0, System timer for time-of-day, disk time-out, and other system timing functions.
1	1	DRAM refresh requests.
1	2	Speaker.
2	0	Fail-safe timer. Connected to the CPU, it generates NMI interrupts at a regular interval to keep the system from locking up.
2	1	Not used.
2	2	Available for manufacturer-dependent timing functions.

Direct Memory Access (DMA)

The EISA computer systems provides four types of cycles used to transfer data between the DMA device and the computer's memory. These are:

> ISA-compatible cycle
>
> Type A cycle
>
> Type B cycle
>
> Burst DMA cycle

ISA-Compatible Cycles

The ISA-compatible cycles are the same for all types of memory, EISA memory and non-EISA memory. The MRDC~ and MWTC~ signal lines allow ISA-type memory to be accessed (unless the address is greater than 16 megabytes and EISA memory responds).

Type A Cycles

Type A cycles can perform 8-, 16-, or 32-bit data transfers between memory and the DMA device in 6 BCLK cycles per transfer. Most

ISA-compatible DMA devices will transfer the data faster (by a factor of 1.3) by using the type A transfer since the type A transfer reduces the duration of the IORC~ or IOWC~ command strobes. Note that this cycle only works with fast EISA memory, and automatically reverts to slower bus timing with non-EISA memory or if data size translation is required.

Type B Cycles

Type B can perform 8-, 16-, or 32-bit data transfers between memory and the DMA device in 4 BCLK cycles per transfer. Most ISA-compatible DMA devices will transfer the data faster (by a factor of 2) by using the type B transfer, reducing the data setup times for I/O writes and the read access time for I/O reads. Note that this cycle only works with fast EISA memory, and automatically reverts to slower bus timing with non-EISA memory or if data size translation is required.

Burst DMA Cycles

Burst DMA cycles (also called Type C cycles) can perform 8-, 16-, or 32-bit data transfers between memory and the DMA device in 1 BCLK cycles per transfer. This is the fastest form of DMA data transfer (31.6MB per second). This is approximately 15 times the data transfer rate of the old ISA-compatible data transfer rate (2.07MB per second).

Input/Output (I/O)

Table 5-4 is a general compilation of the I/O addresses as used by various manufacturers for their ISA and EISA computers. If you are planning to use this data for a product, verify these addresses with your intended target computer systems. Note that all the I/O addresses are shown with their hex values.

TABLE 5-4 I/O Address Map

I/O Address	ISA or EISA	Function
0	ISA	DMA Ch. 0 Address
1	ISA	DMA Ch. 0 Count
2	ISA	DMA Ch. 1 Address
3	ISA	DMA Ch. 1 Count
4	ISA	DMA Ch. 2 Address
5	ISA	DMA Ch. 2 Count
6	ISA	DMA Ch. 3 Address
7	ISA	DMA Ch. 3 Count
8	ISA	DMA Ch. 0–3
9	ISA	DMA Ch. 0–3
A	ISA	DMA Ch. 0–3
B	ISA	DMA Ch. 0–3
C	ISA	DMA Ch. 0–3
D	ISA	DMA Ch. 0–3
E	ISA	DMA Ch. 0–3
F	ISA	DMA Ch. 0–3
10-1F	ISA	Reserved by various manufacturers.
20	ISA	Int. Cont. No.1: IRQ <7:0> Control Register
21	ISA	Int. Cont. No.1: IRQ <7:0> Mask Register
22-3F	ISA	Reserved by various manufacturers.
40	ISA	PI Timer No.1: Counter 0 System Clock
41	ISA	PI Timer No.1: Counter 1 Refresh Request
42	ISA	PI Timer No.1: Counter 2 Speaker Tone
43	ISA	PI Timer No.1 Command Mode Register
44-47	ISA	Reserved by various manufacturers.
48	EISA	PI Timer No.2: Counter 0 Fail-Safe Timer
49		Reserved by various manufacturers.
4A	EISA	PI Timer No.2: Counter 2
4B	EISA	PI Timer No.2 Command Mode Register

TABLE 5-4 **Continued**

I/O Address	ISA or EISA	Function
4C-5F	ISA	Reserved by various manufacturers.
60	ISA	8042 Keyboard/Mouse Controller Data Register
61	ISA	Non-Maskable Interrupt Status Register
62-63	ISA	Reserved by various manufacturers.
64	ISA	8042 Keyboard/Mouse Controller
65-6F	ISA	Reserved by various manufacturers.
70	ISA	Real-Time Clock/CMOS RAM
71	ISA	Real-Time Clock/CMOS RAM
72-80	ISA	Reserved by various manufacturers.
81	ISA	DMA Low Page Register, 8-bit DMA Ch. 2
82	ISA	DMA Low Page Register, 8-bit DMA Ch. 3
83	ISA	DMA Low Page Register, 8-bit DMA Ch. 1
84-86	ISA	Reserved by various manufacturers.
87	ISA	DMA Low Page Register, 8-bit DMA Ch. 0
88	ISA	Reserved by various manufacturers.
89	ISA	DMA Low Page Register, 16-bit DMA Ch. 6
8A	ISA	DMA Low Page Register, 16-bit DMA Ch. 7
8B	ISA	DMA Low Page Register, 16-bit DMA Ch. 5
8C-8E	ISA	Reserved by various manufacturers.
8F	ISA	DMA Low Page Register
90-91	ISA	Reserved by various manufacturers.
92	HP ISA	CMOS Password Lock Enable
9A-9F	ISA	Reserved by various manufacturers.
A0	ISA	Int. Cont. No.2
A1	ISA	Int. Cont. No.1
A2-BF	ISA	Reserved by various manufacturers.
C0	ISA	DMA Ch. 4

TABLE 5-4   Continued

I/O Address	ISA or EISA	Function
C1	ISA	Reserved by various manufacturers.
C2	ISA	DMA Ch. 4
C3	ISA	Reserved by various manufacturers.
C4	ISA	DMA Ch. 5 Address (DREQ5)
C5	ISA	Reserved by various manufacturers.
C6	ISA	DMA Ch. 5 Count
C7	ISA	Reserved by various manufacturers.
C8	ISA	DMA Ch. 6 Address (DREQ6)
C9	ISA	Reserved by various manufacturers.
CA	ISA	DMA Ch. 6 Count
CB	ISA	Reserved by various manufacturers.
CC	ISA	DMA Ch. 7 Address (DREQ7)
CD	ISA	Reserved by various manufacturers.
CE	ISA	DMA Ch. 7 Count
CF	ISA	Reserved by various manufacturers.
D0	ISA	DMA Ch. 4–7
D1	ISA	Reserved by various manufacturers.
D2	ISA	DMA Ch. 4–7
D3	ISA	Reserved by various manufacturers.
D4	ISA	DMA Ch. 4–7
D5	ISA	Reserved by various manufacturers.
D6	ISA	DMA Ch. 4–7
D7	ISA	Reserved by various manufacturers.
D8	ISA	DMA Ch. 4–7
D9	ISA	Reserved by various manufacturers.
DA	ISA	DMA Ch. 4–7
DB	ISA	Reserved by various manufacturers.
DC	ISA	DMA Ch. 4–7

TABLE 5-4   Continued

I/O Address	ISA or EISA	Function
DD	ISA	Reserved by various manufacturers.
DE	ISA	DMA Ch. 4–7
DF-EF	ISA	Reserved by various manufacturers.
F0	ISA	Clear Math Coprocessor Port
F1	ISA	Reset Math Coprocessor
F2-1EF	ISA	Reserved by various manufacturers.
1F0-1F8	ISA	Primary Hard Disk Registers
1F9-1FF	ISA	Reserved by various manufacturers.
200-207	ISA	Game Controller Registers
208-277	ISA	Reserved by various manufacturers.
278-27F	ISA	Parallel Port 2
280-2F7	ISA	Reserved by various manufacturers.
2F8-2FF	ISA	Serial Port 2
300-31F	ISA	Prototype Card
320-377	ISA	Reserved by various manufacturers.
378-37F	ISA	Parallel Port 1
380-38F	ISA	Synchronous Data Link
390-39F	ISA	Reserved by various manufacturers.
3A0-3AF	ISA	Bisynchronous 1 Registers
3B0-3BF	ISA	Monochrome Display/Printer Expander Boards
3C0-3CF	ISA	Enhanced Graphics Adapter Registers
3D0-3DF	ISA	Color/Graphics Expander Board
3E0-3E7	ISA	Reserved by various manufacturers.
3E8-3EF	ISA	Serial Port 3
3F0-3F7	ISA	Primary Floppy Disk Controller
3F8-3FF	ISA	Serial Port 1
400	EISA	Reserved
401	EISA	DMA Ch. 0

TABLE 5-4   Continued

I/O Address	ISA or EISA	Function
402	EISA	Reserved
403	EISA	DMA Ch. 1
404	EISA	Reserved
405	EISA	DMA Ch. 2
406	EISA	Reserved
407	EISA	DMA Ch. 3
408-409	EISA	Reserved
40A	EISA	DMA Ch. 0–3
40B	EISA	DMA Ch. 0–3
40C	EISA	Host/EISA Bus Master Control Register
40D-460	EISA	Reserved
461	EISA	Extended NMI Status Port
462	EISA	Software NMI Register
463	EISA	Undefined
464	EISA	EISA Bus Master
465	EISA	EISA Bus Master
466-480	EISA	Reserved by various manufacturers.
481	EISA	DMA High Page Register, DMA Ch. 2
482	EISA	DMA High Page Register, DMA Ch. 3
483	EISA	DMA High Page Register, DMA Ch. 1
484-486	EISA	Reserved by various manufacturers.
487	EISA	DMA High Page Register, DMA Ch. 0
488	EISA	Reserved by various manufacturers.
489	EISA	DMA High Page Register, DMA Ch. 6
48A	EISA	DMA High Page Register, DMA Ch. 7
48B	EISA	DMA High Page Register, DMA Ch. 5
48C-48E	EISA	Reserved by various manufacturers.
48F	EISA	DMA High Page Register

TABLE 5-4   Continued

I/O Address	ISA or EISA	Function
490-4C5	EISA	Reserved by various manufacturers.
4C6	EISA	DMA Ch. 5 High Word Count
4C7-4C9	EISA	Undefined
4CA	EISA	DMA Ch. 6 High Word Count
4CB	EISA	DMA Ch. 4–7
4CC-4CD	EISA	Undefined
4CE	EISA	DMA Ch. 7 High Word Count
4CF	EISA	Undefined
4D0	EISA	Int. Cont. No.1: IRQ 7:0
4D1	EISA	Int. Cont. No.2: IRQ 15:8
4D2	EISA	Reserved by various manufacturers.
4D3	EISA	Reserved by various manufacturers.
4D4	EISA	DMA Ch. 4–7
4D5	EISA	Reserved by various manufacturers.
4D6	EISA	DMA Ch. 4–7
4D7-4DF	EISA	Reserved by various manufacturers.
4E0	EISA	DMA Ch. 0
4E1	EISA	DMA Ch. 0
4E2	EISA	DMA Ch. 0
4E3	EISA	Reserved by various manufacturers.
4E4	EISA	DMA Ch. 1
4E5	EISA	DMA Ch. 1
4E6	EISA	DMA Ch. 1
4E7	EISA	Reserved by various manufacturers.
4E8	EISA	DMA Ch. 2
4E9	EISA	DMA Ch. 2
4EA	EISA	DMA Ch. 2
4EB	EISA	Reserved by various manufacturers.
4EC	EISA	DMA Ch. 3

TABLE 5-4   Continued

I/O Address	ISA or EISA	Function
4ED	EISA	DMA Ch. 3
4EE	EISA	DMA Ch. 3
4EF-4F3	EISA	Reserved by various manufacturers.
4F4	EISA	DMA Ch. 5
4F5	EISA	DMA Ch. 5
4F6	EISA	DMA Ch. 5
4F7	EISA	Reserved by various manufacturers.
4F8	EISA	8237-CP: DMA Ch. 6
4F9	EISA	DMA Ch. 6
4FA	EISA	DMA Ch. 6
4FB	EISA	Reserved by various manufacturers.
4FC	EISA	DMA Ch. 7
4FD	EISA	DMA Ch. 7
4FE	EISA	DMA Ch. 7
4FF	EISA	Reserved by various manufacturers.
500-7FF	EISA	Alias of 100-3FF
800-8FF	EISA	CMOS RAM
900-BFF	EISA	Alias of 100-3FF
C00	EISA	CMOS RAM Page Select Port
C01-C02	EISA	Undefined
C03	EISA	Cache Control Port
C04-C39	EISA	Undefined
C40	EISA	Hard and Floppy Disk Controllers, Parallel Port, Mouse Port
C41	EISA	Serial Port
C42	EISA	Reserved
C43-C79	EISA	Undefined
C80-C82	EISA	Processor PCA Board Identification Bytes
C83	EISA	Reserved by various manufacturers.

TABLE 5-4 Continued

I/O Address	ISA or EISA	Function
C84	EISA	Processor PCA Board Enable
C85-FFF	EISA	Reserved by various manufacturers.
1000-10FF	EISA	Slot 1
1100-13FF	EISA	Alias of 100-3FF
1400-14FF	EISA	Slot 1
1500-17FF	EISA	Alias of 100-3FF
1800-18FF	EISA	Slot 1
1900-1BFF	EISA	Alias of 100-3FF
1C00-1CFF	EISA	Slot 1
1D00-1FFF through	EISA	Alias of 100-3FF
8000-80FF	EISA	Slot 8
8100-83FF	EISA	Alias of 100-3FF
8400-84FF	EISA	Slot 8
8500-87FF	EISA	Alias of 100-3FF
8800-88FF	EISA	Slot 8
8900-8BFF	EISA	Alias of 100-3FF
8C00-8CFF	EISA	Slot 8
8D00-8FFF	EISA	Alias of 100-3FF
9FFF-FFFF	EISA	Undefined

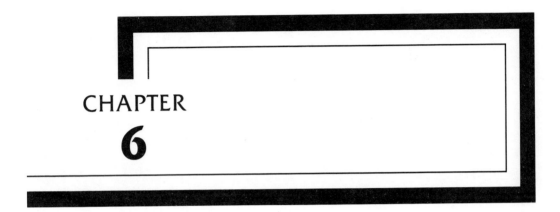

CHAPTER
6

EISA Software

This chapter covers the software that is specific to the EISA computers. There are two types of software covered here: programs that are run in order to set up (configure) and use the computer, and files that contain the configuration data from which the computer performs the configuration process.

Since each of the dozens of manufacturers designing EISA computers will be providing software for installing and configuring their systems, this chapter cannot hope to address the use of each of these systems. I have therefore taken the approach that most of the manufacturers will adhere to the EISA specification. Another possibility is that some software developers will come up with installation programs that will work on several different computer systems, and will sell their software either to hardware developers or directly to the public. In addition, a public domain version is also possible. Since this book is being written and published at the time when the developers are in the process of analyzing EISA and their plans to fit into the EISA world, it is not possible to tell you what they will do, only what they might do, and what the EISA specification defines and allows them to do.

One of the first things that any system will need is a configuration utility more powerful than the SETUP and CONFIGURATION utilities of today. Today's utilities park the heads of a disk drive, set the number and types of drives, set the date and time, and set the video type. They then store this information in CMOS memory. The EISA configuration utility does all of the above, in addition to providing system configuration information on all of the cards, both EISA and ISA, that are plugged into the system.

EISA Configuration

Configuration Utility

The MS-DOS based EISA configuration utility program replaces the old setup utilities offered by computer manufacturers and provides functions such as the generation of system configuration information for the programmable EISA I/O boards. Since EISA computers also support ISA boards, the utility provides I/O board jumper and switch-setting information. This saves a user the time and frustration associated with configuring ISA boards. Once the configuration utility has been run, the resulting information is stored in nonvolatile memory. In this way, the utility need be run only once, when setting up the computer, and not each time the power is turned on or the computer is reset.

The EISA configuration utility configures the computer's CMOS memory to match the expansion cards installed in the system. This utility has been developed by Hewlett-Packard and Compaq and will be distributed in some form to each of the manufacturers. They may, in turn, make certain modifications to the program to tailor it to their individual needs. Because of the changes that each of the manufacturers may make, it is not possible to present the program in a final form. A generic version is presented here. The version you will be using may differ slightly.

When the utility initially comes up on the screen, it displays a welcome screen telling the user the name of the manufacturer, and any other particulars the manufacturer feels necessary. Several screens of information about the utility, how to use it, and perhaps manufacturer-specific information are then presented, followed by a System Configuration Menu.

System Configuration Menu

Typically, the System Configuration Menu will typically have the appearance of a Windows application, with five headings across the top of the screen: System, Edit, View, Settings, and Help.

A list of the function keys that can be used will appear below these, and below that, a list of the boards presently in the system. The contents of the screen will be similar to the example in Figure 6-1.

Note that the sample screen shows more than 25 lines. There will be a "scroll bar" at the right side of the screen that will allow you to move up and down to view the eight slots. Some computers will have fewer than 8 slots, and some may have more, so the use of the scroll bar may vary from system to system.

As you select each one of the five pull-down topics from across the top of the screen, you will get a menu of different func-

```
System    Edit    View    Settings    Help
```

These are the options detected by your computer. If this information is correct, select Exit from the System pull-down menu.

Press [F10] to activate the menu bar.
Press [F1] at any time to display help information.
Press [Shift+F1] at any time to display an index of help topics.

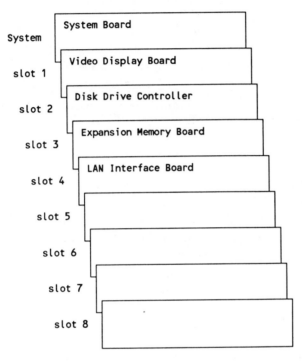

```
System      System Board

slot 1          Video Display Board

slot 2          Disk Drive Controller

slot 3          Expansion Memory Board

slot 4          LAN Interface Board

slot 5

slot 6

slot 7

slot 8
```

```
[F10]=Menu bar    [F1]=Help    [Shift+F1]=Help topics    Tab
```

FIGURE 6-1   The System Configuration Menu

tions you can perform. These are summarized in the following paragraphs.

System Menu

Open   Used to open an existing SCI file that contains preset configuration information.

Save As   Used to save a configuration in a file for later use.

Print	Used to print the existing system configuration information.
Verify	Used to verify the existing system configuration information to make sure there are no resource conflicts.
Exit	Used to exit from the program.

Edit Menu

Add	Used to add a board or option to the system configuration.
Move	Used to move a board from one slot to another.
Remove	Used to remove a board from the system.
Change function	Used to change the function of a board when you are viewing it in a detailed mode.
Change resource	Used to change the resources of a board when you are viewing it in a detailed mode.
Revert to saved	Used to revert to the previously saved version of the configuration.
Reset to defaults	Used to reset the system configuration to the manufacturers default values.
Lock	Used to lock a board or a system configuration.
Unlock	Used to unlock a previously locked system or board.

View Menu

Overview	Displays an overview of the system showing which boards are in each slot. Selecting a board provides more detailed information.
Detailed by slot	Displays information on the system, presented slot-by-slot.
Detailed by type	Displays information on the system, sorted by type of information.

Switch & jumper settings	Displays the switch and jumper settings for the selected board.
Software parameters	Displays the software parameters for the board.
Connections	Displays information on cabling between the board and any interconnected peripherals.
Board specifications	Displays a list of the board's specifications.
Resources	Displays the interrupt, I/O, and memory information on the selected board.

Settings Menu

Auto verify	Causes the computer to check for resource conflicts each time a change is made.
Manual verify	Causes the verification process to be delayed until the Verify option is selected from the System pull-down.

Help Menu

Help topics	Lists the topics on which help is available.
Help	Provides general information on the help function.
How to use keys	Provides information on how to use the various function keys used in the configuration utility program.
How to use help	Provides a screen of information on how to use the help function.
Copyright information	Provides copyright and revision information on the configuration utility program.

Nonvolatile Memory

EISA computers have EISA nonvolatile memory as well as standard ISA nonvolatile memory. The configuration utility uses EISA nonvolatile memory to store information about the boards installed in the system. This information includes which I/O ports are used by the board, which DMA addresses are used, and which IRQs are needed.

The configuration utility uses the ISA nonvolatile memory for storing configuration information, including the system disk drive types, the video adapter type, and amount of memory installed.

Configuration (CFG) Files

CFG files are needed for both ISA and EISA I/O boards. The configuration utility uses the information contained in the CFG files to determine the system resources each board requires. This information helps a user resolve any resource conflicts that may occur if multiple boards require similar resources. By using a combination of function and choice statements, the manufacturer creates a list of configuration options that correspond to the selectable resources for the board.

CFG Filename Format

CFG filenames must adhere to the following format: !vvvpppp.CFG, where vvv is a three character vendor identification number, pppp is a 4-hex-character vendor product identification number, and .CFG is the file extension.

The following examples are valid CFG filenames:

    !ABC1234.CFG
    !VND0015.CFG
    !PAR0C15.CFG
    !LAD26AF.CFG

CFG File Format

CFG files are ASCII files that adhere to the CFG language. CFG files can be created using a text editor or an MS-DOS based CFG creation utility supplied by some manufacturers. CFG files are divided into blocks. The first block is the board identification block containing I/O board and slot type information. The second block is the initialization identification block containing I/O port initialization information and switch and jumper configuration information.

The third and following blocks are the function identification blocks. These contain user-selectable I/O board information presented to the user by the configuration utility. Refer to the "Brief CFG Description" below for an overview of the CFG language. Explanations of the language are given as part of the example CFG files following this brief description.

Brief CFG Description

```
[ ]      - Square brackets indicate optional items.

BOARD
        ID = "vvvpppp"
        NAME = "name"
        MFR = "name"
        CATEGORY = "category"
        [SLOT= ISA/ISA16/ISA8OR16/OTHER/EISA/VIR/EMB[n] ]
        [LENGTH = value]
        [AMPERAGE = value]
        [SKIRT = YES/NO]
        [READID = YES/NO]
        [BUSMASTER = value]
        [IOCHECK = VALID/INVALID]
        [DISABLE = SUPPORTED/UNSUPPORTED]
        [COMMENTS = "comment text"]
        [HELP = "help text"]

IOPORT(x) = address
        [SIZE = BYTE/WORD/DWORD]
        [INITVAL = [LOC(list)]]

SWITCH(x) = value
        NAME = "description"
        STYPE = DIP/ROTARY/SLIDE
        [VERTICAL = YES/NO]
        [REVERSE = YES/NO]
```

```
                    [LABEL = LOC(list) list]
                    [INITVAL = LOC(list) list]
                    [COMMENTS = "comment text"]
                    [HELP = "help text"]


        JUMPER(x) = value
                    NAME = "description"
                    JTYPE = INLINE/PAIRED/TRIPOLE
                    [VERTICAL = YES/NO]
                    [REVERSE = YES/NO]
                    [LABEL = LOC(list) list]
                    [INITVAL = LOC(list) list]
                    [FACTORY = LOC(list) list]
                    [COMMENTS = "comment text"]
                    [HELP = "help text"]


        [GROUP = "name"]


        FUNCTION = "name"
                    [TYPE = "type"]
                    [COMMENTS = "comment text"]
                    [CONNECTION = "connection text"]
                    [HELP = "help text"]
                    CHOICE = "name"
                            LINK/FREE/COMBINE
                            [SUBTYPE = "name"]
                            [DISABLE = YES/NO]
                            [AMPERAGE = value]
                            [TOTALMEM = list [STEP = value]]
                            [MEMORY = size]
                            [ADDRESS = value]
                            [WRITABLE = YES/NO]
                            [MEMTYPE = value]
                            [SIZE = BYTE/WORD/DWORD]
                            [DECODE = 20/24/32]
                            [CACHE = YES/NO]
                            [SHARE = YES/NO/"test"]
                            [DMA = list]
                                    [SHARE = YES/NO/"test"]
                                    [SIZE = BYTE/WORD/DWORD]
                                    [TIMING = DEFAULT/TYPEA/TYPEB/TYPEC]
```

```
                          [PORT = list]
                                  [SHARE = YES/NO/"test"]
                                  [SIZE = BYTE/WORD/DWORD]
                          [IRQ = list]
                                  [SHARE = YES/NO/"test"]
                                  [TRIGGER = LEVEL/EDGE]
                          [INIT = value]

                          [SUBCHOICE]
                                  [DISABLE = YES/NO]
                                  [AMPERAGE = value]
                                  [TOTALMEM = list [STEP = value]]

                               .
                               .
                               .

              [SUBFUNCTION = "name"]
                          [TYPE = "type"]
                          [CONNECTION = "comment text"]
                          [COMMENTS = "comment text"]
                          [HELP = "help text"]
                          CHOICE = "name"
                                  [
                                              ]
                               .
                               .
                               .
                  [CHOICE = "name"]
                               .
                               .
                               .
                  [CHOICE = "name"]

      [ENDGROUP]

      [INCLUDE = "vvvpppp.OVL"]
```

CFG File Examples

ISA Serial Board   A company called Zap Computer Systems produces a small ISA board with one serial port that can be configured as COM1 or COM2. A switch is used to select the COM port as follows:

$$
\begin{array}{c}
\text{switch} \\
\underline{1}
\end{array}
$$

$$
\text{positions:} \quad
\begin{array}{ll}
0 & = \text{COM1} \\
1 & = \text{COM2}
\end{array}
$$

This board is the first produced by the company so they decide on a board product number of 0000. Their vendor identification number is ZAP so the CFG filename is !ZAP0000.CFG. The CFG file for the Zap serial board follows.

```
;A comment line - comments are delimited by a ";"
;
; Following is the board identification block.  The board ID is
; given.  Note the similarities with the CFG filename.  The name
; of the board and manufacturer come next.  The category COM
; indicates this board is used for communications.  The length
; of the board is 330 millimeters and it is an 8-bit ISA board.
;
BOARD
        ID = "ZAP0000"
        NAME = "Zap Serial Board"
        MFR = "Zap Computer Systems"
        CATEGORY = "COM"
        SLOT = ISA8
        LENGTH = 330
;
; Next comes the initialization identification block.  Only a
; SWITCH statement is used for the Zap serial board CFG file.
; The SWITCH statement information defines the board switches.
; The switch name, type, and board label are given.
;
SWITCH(1) = 1
        NAME = "COM Port Selection"
        STYPE = DIP
        LABEL = LOC(1) "Switch 1"
;
; Now comes the function identification block.  The Zap serial
; board CFG file has only one function, however, most CFG files
; will contain several.  The function for serial port 1 has two
; choices, COM1 or COM2.  These choices are presented to a user
; by the configuration utility.  The configuration utility keeps
```

```
; track of the user's selection by storing the resource
; information below the choice in EISA nonvolatile memory.  For
; example, if the user selects COM2, the utility knows that IRQ 3
; and I/O ports 02F8h-02FFh are used by the board.  The LINK
; statement is used because the resources are related.
;

    FUNCTION = "Serial Port 1"
        TYPE = "COM,ASY"
        CHOICE = "COM1"
                SUBTYPE = "COM1"
                    LINK
                        IRQ = 4
                        PORT = 03F8h-03FFh


        CHOICE = "COM2"
                SUBTYPE = "COM2"
                    LINK
                        IRQ = 3
                        PORT = 02F8h-02FFh
```

EISA Serial/Parallel Board   Zap Computer Systems decided to create an EISA version of the serial board. Zap also decided to add a second serial port and a parallel port to the board. The board will not have any switches but instead will have one programmable I/O port. The new EISA serial/parallel board CFG filename is ZAP0010.CFG.

Programmable I/O port definition:

```
Port 0zC40h:

        Bit 0 - Parallel port number (0=LPT1, 1=LPT2)
        Bit 1 - Enable parallel port (1=enable)
        Bit 2 - Serial port 1 number (0=COM1, 1=COM2)
        Bit 3 - Enable serial port 1 (1=enable)
        Bit 4 - Serial port 2 number (0=COM1, 1=COM2)
        Bit 5 - Enable serial port 2 (1=enable)
        Bit 6 - reserved
        Bit 7 - reserved
```

The CFG file for the Zap serial/parallel board would be:

```
;
; The board identification block below shows the board ID, the name,
; and the manufacturer.  MFC indicates this board is a multi-function
; board.  The length of the board is 330 millimeters and it is of type
; EISA.
;

BOARD
        ID = "ZAP0010"
        NAME = "Zap Serial/Parallel Board"
        MFR = "Zap Computer Systems"
        CATEGORY = "MFC"
        SLOT = EISA
        LENGTH = 330


;
; This is the initialization identification block. The IOPORT statement
; replaces the SWITCH statement from the ISA board example and is defined
; for use later in the CFG file.  The Z tells the configuration utility
; to replace that position with the slot number in which the board is
; installed.  This way the CFG text does not need to be changed no
; matter what slot the board is in.  The xxxxxxxb means the initial
; value of the port will be filled in later by the configuration utility
; based on what choices the user makes.
;
IOPORT(1) = 0ZC40h
        SIZE = BYTE
        INITVAL = xxxxxxxb


;
; This is the function identification block.  This example has added a
; GROUP statement.  This is done to group common functions together.
; The other new statement used is the INIT statement.  The INIT value
; that corresponds to a choice is stored in EISA nonvolatile memory by
; the configuration utility.  At system power-on, the BIOS looks for
; INIT entries in EISA nonvolatile memory and properly initializes the
; hardware to match what the user has selected.  All function in a
; group are enclosed between the GROUP and ENDGROUP statements.
;
```

```
GROUP = "Serial Ports"
        TYPE = "COM,ASY"
     FUNCTION = "Serial Port 1"
        TYPE = "P1"
        CHOICE = "COM1"
                  SUBTYPE = "COM1"
                  LINK
                         IRQ = 4
                         PORT = 03F8h-03FFh
                         INIT = IOPORT(1) xxxx10xx
        CHOICE = "COM2"
                  SUBTYPE = "COM2"
                  LINK
                         IRQ = 3
                         PORT = 02F8h-02FFh
                         INIT = IOPORT(1) xxxx11xx
        CHOICE = "Disable"
                  DISABLE = YES
                  FREE
                         INIT = IOPORT(1) xxxx0xxx

     FUNCTION = "Serial Port 2"
        TYPE = "P2"
        CHOICE = "COM1"
                  SUBTYPE = "COM1"
                  LINK
                         IRQ = 4
                         PORT = 03F8h-03FFh
                         INIT = IOPORT(1) xx10xxxx
        CHOICE = "COM2"
                  SUBTYPE = "COM2"
                  LINK
                         IRQ = 3
                         PORT = 02F8h-02FFh
                         INIT = IOPORT(1) xx11xxxx
        ;
        ; The FREE statement is used because
        ; no related resources exist.
        ;
        CHOICE = "Disable"
                  DISABLE = YES
                  FREE
                  INIT = IOPORT(1) xx0xxxxx
```

```
ENDGROUP
;
    FUNCTION = "Parallel Port 1"
        TYPE = "PAR"
        CHOICE = "LPT1"
                SUBTYPE = "LPT1"
                LINK
                        IRQ = 7
                        PORT = 0378h-037Fh
                        INIT = IOPORT(1) xxxxxx10
        CHOICE = "LPT2"
                SUBTYPE = "LPT2"
                LINK
                        IRQ = 5
                        PORT = 0278h-027Fh
                        INIT = IOPORT(1) xxxxxx11
        CHOICE = "Disable"
                DISABLE = YES
                FREE
                        INIT = IOPORT(1) xxxxxx0x
```

EISA VGA Video Board   Zap computer systems also produces an EISA version of a VGA video board. The CFG name is !ZAP0020.CFG and the text is shown below.

```
; The board identification block is similar to the previous CFG examples
; with the exception of the category.  VID indicates this is a
; video board.

BOARD
ID = "ZAP0020"
NAME = "Zap Systems VGA Board"
MFR = "Zap Computer Systems"
CATEGORY = "VID"
SLOT = EISA
LENGTH = 330
READID = YES


;
; No initialization block for this board
;
```

```
;
; The function identification block has one function that merely
; defines the board resources.  MEMORY statements are used to let
; the configuration utility know where the board ROM and RAM resides.
;
FUNCTION = "Video Board Operation"
  TYPE = "VID"
  CHOICE = "Primary VGA adapter"
    SUBTYPE = "VGA"
    FREE
      MEMORY = 64K
        ADDRESS = 0A0000h      ;Board video RAM area
        WRITABLE = YES
        MEMTYPE = OTHER
        CACHE = NO             ;Memory not cachable
        SHARE = NO             ;Memory not sharable

      MEMORY = 32K
        ADDRESS = 0C0000h      ;Board video ROM area
        WRITABLE = NO
        MEMTYPE = OTHER
        CACHE = NO             ;Memory not cachable
        SHARE = NO             ;Memory not sharable
```

Overlay (OVL) Files

Anticipating that not all boards could be described adequately with the configuration language, overlay files were created to provide extensions to the CFG language.

An overlay file, commonly referred to as an OVL, is a piece of executable code that provides configuration capabilities beyond the scope of the configuration language. Written in a combination of C and 80x86 assembly language, OVL files conform to the MS-DOS executable file format. The difference between an OVL and a stand-alone program is the strict communication interface the OVL adheres to. This is described later.

Most commonly, OVLs assist in the autoconfiguration process. In an EISA computer, autoconfiguration generally refers to the ability to select system options without having to prompt the user for input. For example, when the configuration utility encounters

two boards that have serial ports, it automatically assigns one to
COM1 and the other to COM2. This kind of autoconfiguration is
easy for the utility to perform, since it has a list of possible COM
choices for both serial ports and it can simply select a unique choice
for each port. Naturally, the choices selected by the utility can be
overridden. In most cases, however, the default choices selected by
the utility are acceptable.

Consider another common example. Most PCs have at least
one flexible disk drive, usually a 3.5-inch or 5.25-inch drive. Tra-
ditionally, one of the first steps in configuring a PC is to describe
the type of flexible disk drive attached. But suppose the PC included in its hardware design a mechanism for identifying the type
of disk drives attached? The manufacturer could then write an OVL
to interrogate the hardware and select the configuration choices on
behalf of the utility, no longer requiring the user to enter the drive
type. This is another example of autoconfiguration possible with
an EISA computer.

OVLs can range from simple to complex. They can be used
simply to provide CFG text for management by the configuration
utility, or they can be so complex as to take complete control over
the screens presented to the user.

Although all boards must have a CFG file, the OVL file is
optional; the decision to include an OVL file is up to the board
manufacturer. The one exception to this rule is the system board.
In an EISA computer, the system board must have an OVL to
configure the ISA nonvolatile memory, since the configuration utility does not provide this functionality. Toward the end of the configuration process, the system board OVL looks at the information
stored in EISA nonvolatile memory by the configuration utility to
determine how to configure ISA nonvolatile memory.

OVL File Structure

When the configuration utility loads a CFG file into the system
configuration, it checks for an INCLUDE="xxxyyyy.OVL" statement. This statement may occur anywhere in the CFG file following
the board identification block. It tells the utility that the CFG file
has an accompanying OVL file that is to be loaded into memory.

To understand how an OVL operates, it is first necessary to identify the three major phases of system configuration provided by the utility. Taken from a broad perspective, the configuration utility does three things. First, when loading, it examines the system and creates an image of the system configuration. Beginning with the system board, it automatically loads in CFG files for all EISA cards and any ISA cards previously configured and saved in EISA CMOS. This is known as the *initialization* phase.

Second, the user interacts with the utility, changing resources or function choices if necessary. The utility keeps track of any changes made and may verify and resolve resource conflicts. Collectively, this is known as the *edit* phase.

Third, when all changes have been made and the system configuration is complete, the user may save the configuration and exit the utility. This updates the system's EISA and ISA nonvolatile memory. This is known as the *update* phase. While it is impossible to completely separate these three phases in the configuration utility, an OVL is written very specifically to function in only one phase at any given time.

An OVL is an extension to the configuration capability of the standard configuration utility. At all times, it should be transparent to the user that he is interacting with OVL-specific code. Also, an OVL has access to the same screen interface library used by the utility. This library should be utilized to achieve a consistent look-and-feel with the configuration utility if the OVL is complex enough to require it.

To describe an OVL in the simplest of terms, it consists of three functions that are invoked at a specific time during the configuration process. Actually, the utility invokes the OVL code through a single entry point. The utility passes to the OVL a set of common parameters that describe the current status of the configuration process. The OVL modifies some of the parameters to return information to the utility. For each call to the OVL, the same parameter structure is used. This method of parameter passing is referred to as a common stack frame.

OVL Example

To better understand how OVLs work, let's construct one OVL for a simple expanded memory card. Assume the card can hold up to

2MB of RAM in 512K increments. This means there are four possible memory configuration choices for the card. First, start with a simple .CFG file for the board, shown below.

```
BOARD
  ID = "ZAP1000"
  NAME = "Zap Expanded Memory Card"
  MFR = "Zap Technologies"
  CATEGORY = "MEM"
  SLOT = EISA
  READID = YES
  COMMENTS = "The Zap Memory Expansion board lets you add extra memory
  to your system."

FUNCTION = "Memory Size"
  COMMENTS = "This choice controls the amount of memory installed on
  your Zap memory board."
    TYPE = "MEM"
      CHOICE = "Expanded Memory"
        SUBCHOICE
          LINK
            MEMORY =  0 = 2M STEP = 512K
            MEMTYPE = EXP
```

Given the CFG text above, this card does not require an OVL file. The CFG text adequately describes all the resources on the card. However, by itself, the CFG file cannot determine the amount of memory installed on the card. The user still needs to select the Change Resources function from the utility's Edit panel to set the correct amount of installed memory. The example OVL below illustrates how to make this selection automatically. Note that the term "panel" is used in the EISA specification to refer to the pull-down menus in the various installation and configuration utilities.

First, remove the CFG text for the memory size function from the CFG file and replace it with INCLUDE="ZAP1000.OVL". This instructs the utility to load the OVL file as it loads the CFG file.

```
BOARD
  ID = "ZAP2000"
  NAME = "Zap Expanded Memory Card"
  MFR = "Zap Computer Systems"
  CATEGORY = "MEM"
  SLOT = EISA
  READID = YES
  COMMENTS = "The Zap Memory Expansion board lets you add extra memory
  to your system."

INCLUDE="ZAP2000.OVL"
```

The following OVL written in Microsoft C 5.1 detects the amount of memory installed and selects the proper memory choice for the utility.

```c
#include "ovl.h"      ; Filename: OVL.H

int        DetectMemorySize(void);
void far _OvlCommonEntry( OVL_PARAMETERS );

int _acrtused         = 0;         /* Force linker not to use crt0   */
#define OVL_VERSION     0x0001
#define MEM_CHOICE      0          /* 1st byte in selections[] array */

unsigned char cfgText[] = {
      "FUNCTION = \"Expanded Memory\"\n"
      "COMMENTS = \"Select the amount of memory installed\n"
                "on your Zap memory board.\"\n"
      "HELP = \"Press [Enter] to edit the choice for memory size.\"\n"
      "TYPE = \"MEM\"\n"
        "CHOICE = \"512K\"\n"
              "LINK  MEMORY =  512K  MEMTYPE=EXP\n"
        "CHOICE = \"1024K\"\n"
              "LINK  MEMORY = 1024K  MEMTYPE=EXP\n"
        "CHOICE = \"1536K\"\n"
              "LINK  MEMORY = 1536K  MEMTYPE=EXP\n"
        "CHOICE = \"2048K\"\n"
              "LINK  MEMORY = 2048K  MEMTYPE=EXP\n"
};
```

```
CFG_FUNCTION memorySize = {
        (CFG_FUNCTION *) NULL,        /* Only one function in cfg text */
        { 0, 0, 0 },                  /* Default choice is 512K        */
        0x0000,                       /* OVL will own edit changes     */
        (unsigned char *) NULL,
        (unsigned char *) NULL,
        (unsigned char *) NULL
};

CFG_DATA cfgData = {
         0,
        -1,                           /* let utility determine slot     */
        cfgText,                      /* the cfg text for ovl's function */
        &memorySize,                  /* select memory size function     */
         0
};

void far
_OvlCommonEntry(ovlParameters)        /* Utility will pass control */
OVL_PARAMETERS ovlParameters;         /* to the OVL here...        */
{
    switch( ovlParameters.function ) {
        case FUNCTION_INIT:

            if (ovlParameters.entryStatus & TARGET_MACHINE) {
                memorySize.selections[MEM_CHOICE]=DetectMemorySize();
            }

            /* If memory STR did not change since last time,
               then ovlParameters.exitStatus |=OVL_NO_CHANGES;        */

            ovlParameters.pcfgData   = &cfgData;
            ovlParameters.ovlVersion = OVL_VERSION;
            ovlParameters.exitStatus |= MULTI_SUPPORT;
            break;

        case FUNCTION_CHANGE:
        case FUNCTION_UPDATE:
                ovlParameters.exitStatus = OVL_NO_CHANGES;
            break;
    };
}
int DetectMemorySize()
```

```
{
    /* Four choices: 0=512K, 1=1024K, 2=1536K, and 3=2048K    */
    /* Check the hardware to detect memory size...            */
    /* For this example, let's just assume 1024K is installed. */

    return (1);
}
```

When writing an OVL program, the user must observe a few important rules. Notice the variable _acrtused is declared. This instructs the runtime linker not to link the C runtime module with the OVL's object file. Since the OVL will be running along with the utility, the runtime module will have already been loaded for the utility. Note that without the runtime module, the OVL cannot be run as a stand-alone program.

A second rule when writing OVLs is that the function _OvlCommonEntry must be the first subroutine in the module. This is necessary because the utility will invoke the OVL by transferring control via a far call to the first location in the OVL's code segment. Notice that the function DetectMemorySize() was declared at the top of the program, but not initialized until after function _OvlCommonEntry(). This takes advantage of C's function prototyping capability to satisfy all forward references.

The third rule to observe is that building the .OBJ file requires certain compiler options. The following Microsoft makefile will correctly compile the OVL source code:

```
zap1.obj:       zap1.c ovl.h
                cl -Ox -Zlp -Afus -nologo -c zap.c


zap2000.ovl:    zap1.obj
                link zap1, zap2000.ovl;
```

Accessory card OVLs are limited in size to 16K for both code and data. System board OVLs are limited to 64K in size. All data structures are packed. This is necessary to ensure that the configuration utility has enough free memory to load all CFG and OVL files. Because of this, OVLs are compiled using a small memory model. In addition, both the utility and the support routines it provides require far data pointers. The utility also provides a 4K stack for OVLs to use.

OVL Functions

The utility calls an OVL's `_OvlCommonEntry(ovlParameters)` with three possible function values in `ovlParameters` (INIT, CHANGE, UPDATE). With each function call, the utility passes a set of flags in `entryStatus` to indicate its current status. When returning control to the utility, the OVL passes back its flags in `exitStatus`. It is important that the OVL does *not* keep a local copy of information contained in the ovlParameters structure. This prevents the OVL from getting out of sync with the utility. The utility updates the `ovlParameters` structure before each OVL function call.

OVL Function INIT   Normally, the INIT function is called only once, when the OVL is loaded into memory. During this call, the OVL builds the CFG text for the functions it will be handling. Both CFGs and OVLs use the same configuration language to describe resources and functions for configuration. The only exception is that an OVL can define a free-form data function. This function has no subfunctions or choices; it may have a type and subtype string. Free-form data functions contain up to 204 bytes of information in any format. This data is placed unaltered into EISA nonvolatile memory.

During the INIT function call, the OVL must initialize several parameters in the ovlParameters structure for the utility. The OVL should place its version number in `ovlVersion`. This information will be displayed to the user. The parameter `ovlFinal-MemorySize` controls how much memory the utility reserves for the OVL. A value of 0 means unload the OVL from memory; a value of -1 means use the initial size of the OVL. The OVL must also initialize the CFG Data Area. For each function in the CFG text, the OVL initializes a `CFG_FUNCTION` to describe the selections, choice text, and subtype string for the function.

OVL Function CHANGE   The utility makes a CHANGE call to an OVL whenever the user attempts to edit a function supplied and owned by an OVL. The flag functionOwner in the `CFG_FUNCTION` structure specifies who owns a function (is responsible for edit changes). In the Zap memory board example, the OVL supplied one function and let the utility have ownership for changes. It is common to write a small OVL with an INIT function to automatically select an initial value for a function choice, and then let the utility handle any changes.

When an OVL takes ownership for changes, the utility uses ovlParameters.subfunction to indicate what change should take place. Subfunction `CHANGE_SELECTION` indicates the user wants to change the selected choice for a function. The OVL should open a panel and display the function and its choices. The look-and-feel of the panel should be similar to an edit panel opened by the utility. The user can then use the mouse or keyboard to make changes. The following example is the same OVL modified to take control of editing the choice for memory size.

```
#include "ovl.h"          ; FIlename: OVL.H

int         DetectMemorySize(void);
void far _OvlCommonEntry( OVL_PARAMETERS );

int _acrtused         = 0;          /* Force linker not to use crt0   */
#define OVL_VERSION       0x0001
#define MEM_CHOICE        0          /* 1st byte in selections[] array */
#define BID_OK            1024
#define BID_CANCEL        1025

unsigned char cfgText[] = {
      "FUNCTION = \"Expanded Memory\"\n"
      "COMMENTS = \"Select the amount of memory installed\n"
                "on your Zap memory board.\"\n"
      "HELP = \"Press [Enter] to edit the choice for memory size.\"\n"
      "TYPE = \"MEM\"\n"
  "CHOICE = \"512K\"\n"
              "LINK MEMORY =   512K   MEMTYPE=EXP\n"
        "CHOICE = \"1024K\"\n"
              "LINK MEMORY =  1024K   MEMTYPE=EXP\n"
        "CHOICE = \"1536K\"\n"
              "LINK MEMORY =  1536K   MEMTYPE=EXP\n"
        "CHOICE = \"2048K\"\n"
              "LINK MEMORY =  2048K   MEMTYPE=EXP\n"
```

```
};


CFG_FUNCTION memorySize = {
        (CFG_FUNCTION *) NULL,      /* Only one function in cfg text */
        { 0, 0, 0 },               /* Default choice is 512K        */
        0x0001,                    /* OVL will own edit changes      */
        (unsigned char *) NULL,
        (unsigned char *) NULL,
        (unsigned char *) NULL,
};


CFG_DATA cfgData = {
        0,
        -1,                        /* let utility determine slot     */
        cfgText,                   /* let cfg text for ovl's function */
        &memorySize,               /* select memory size function    */
        0
};


PANEL myPanel;   /* handle for opening edit panel on screen        */
EVENT myEvent;    /* event record to trap user keyboard/mouse action */
unsigned char myChoices[]="512K\n1024K\n1536K\n2048K";
unsigned int theChoice,oldChoice;

PANEL_FIELD myField = {
        (PANEL_FIELD *)NULL,   /* only one field */
        (PANEL_FIELD *)NULL,
        LIST_BOX,              /* display myChoices as a list box   */
        AUTO_PLACE,            /* let utility place panel on screen */
        AUTO_PLACE,
        20,
        "Installed Memory",
        AUTO_PLACE,
        AUTO_PLACE,
        20
        4,                     /* show all four choices in list box */
        &theChoice,
        myChoices,             /* the four memory size choices      */
        (unsigned long)NULL,
        "Select the correct amount of memory installed in your card."
};
```

```
PANEL_GROUP myGroup = {
        (PANEL_GROUP *)   NULL,     /* A group is just a collection */
        (PANEL_GROUP *)   NULL,     /* of related fields.  This     */
        (unsigned char *) NULL,     /* example has only one field.  */
        AUTO_PLACE,
        &myField
};


BUTTON buttonCancel = {
        (BUTTON *)NULL,
        (BUTTON *)NULL,
        "Cancel",
        BID_CANCEL,
        "Press <Cancel> to abort your changes.",
        (unsigned int) NULL,
        0x011b
};


BUTTON buttonOk = {
        &buttonCancel,
        (BUTTON *)NULL,
        "Ok",
        BID_OK,
        "Press <Ok> to accept your changes.",
        (unsigned int) NULL,
        0x1c0d
};


void far
_OvlCommonEntry(ovlParameters)          /* Utility will pass control */
OVL_PARAMETERS ovlParameters;           /* to the OVL here...        */
{

    switch( ovlParameters.function ) {
        case FUNCTION_INIT:

            if (ovlParameters.entryStatus & TARGET_MACHINE) {
                theChoice = DetectMemorySize();
                memorySize.selections[MEM_CHOICE] = theChoice;
            }
```

```
            ovlParameters.pcfgData   = &cfgData;
            ovlParameters.ovlVersion = OVL_VERSION;
            ovlParameters.exitStatus |= MULTI_SUPPORT;
            break;

    case FUNCTION_CHANGE:
        if (ovlParameters.subfunction == CHANGE_SELECTION) {
            oldChoice = theChoice;
            myPanel = ovlParameters.Support (OPEN_PANEL,
                                             DIALOG_PANEL,
                                             DEFAULT_STYLE,
                                             "Expanded Memory",
                                             (ACTION *)NULL,
                                             &myGroup,
                                             &buttonOk );

            ovlParameters.Support( DISPLAY_PANEL, myPanel );
        }

        if (   (ovlParameters.subfunction==CHANGE_SELECTION)
           ||(   (ovlParameters.subfunction==CHANGE_RESULTS)
              &&(ovlParameters.entryStatus
                                     & OVL_CHANGES_OK == 0))) {

            ovlParameters.Support( EDIT_PANEL, myPanel, &myEvent);
            ovlParameters.exitStatus = OVL_NO_CHANGES;

            switch (myEvent.eventID) {
                    case BID_OK:
                        if (oldChoice != theChoice)
                            ovlParameters.exitStatus
                                         &= ~OVL_NO_CHANGES;
                        break;
                    case BID_CANCEL:
                        theChoice = oldChoice;
                         break;
            };
        }
        else
            ovlParameters.exitStatus = OVL_NO_CHANGES;

        if (ovlParameters.exitStatus & OVL_NO_CHANGES) {
            ovlParameters.Support(CLOSE_PANEL, myPanel);
```

```
                memorySize.selections[MEM_CHOICE]=theChoice;
        }
        break;

    case FUNCTION_UPDATE:
        ovlParameters.exitStatus |= OVL_NO_CHANGES;
            break;
    };
}


int DetectMemorySize()
    /* Four choices: 0=512K, 1=1024K, 2=1536K, and 3=2048K    */
    /* Check the hardware to detect memory size...            */
    /* For this example, let's just assume 1024K is installed. */

    return (1);
}
```

This second example shows how very little extra code is required for the OVL to handle the editing of a function. The utility provides a complete set of support functions for handling the displaying and editing of data. The OVL need only set up the data structures, open a panel, and call the edit support function. From that point on, the utility handles all user input from both the keyboard and the mouse. This relieves the OVL from the burden of recreating the windows-like interface of the utility, and allows it to focus specifically on its configuration objectives.

Notice how the two subfunctions, CHANGE_SELECTION and CHANGE_RESULTS, work together. At the beginning of the edit, the utility calls the OVL with CHANGE_SELECTION to say, "The user wants to change the choice for a function. Display a panel listing all the choices and let him choose." The OVL responds by opening a panel and calling the edit support function.

When the user makes a choice, the support function returns an event indicating what the user did. If the user pressed the <Ok> pushbutton to end the edit, the OVL checks to see if a new choice was selected and returns this in exitStatus. This is the OVL's way of saying to the utility, "The user made a change. Is this new choice ok?". The utility examines the new choice and returns with subfunction CHANGE_RESULTS to indicate its approval or disapproval. This continues until the utility accepts the user's choice. If the user does not make a new choice or presses <Cancel>, then nothing is changed and the OVL returns control to the utility.

OVL Function UPDATE   This is last of the three functions that the OVL must support. In comparison to the other two functions, this is the easiest to implement. The utility calls the OVL with this function to indicate the configuration process is complete. For system board OVLs, the subfunction UPDATE_CHECK is the last chance to verify that all system resources have been accounted for. For example, if the system board OVL sees a serial port that has not been claimed by any CFG file or OVL file, then it can claim ownership to make sure that the system configuration includes all resources. This situation can occur when a board is installed that has no CFG file.

For both system board OVLs and accessory card OVLs, the subfunction UPDATE_CONFIGURATION indicates the end of the configuration process. The OVL should release any memory or unchain itself from any interrupts. For most OVLs, there is no action to perform during update, and this call is just a good-bye handshake from the utility. The utility will unload the OVL from memory following the UPDATE_CONFIGURATION call. For system board OVLs, the UPDATE_CONFIGURATION subfunction has a special meaning. Remember that EISA computers have two sets of nonvolatile memory. This subfunction signals the system board OVL to go ahead and initialize the ISA-specific nonvolatile memory. This is done by searching through the EISA nonvolatile memory and extracting the necessary information from the TYPE and SUB-TYPE strings defined for each function. During its search, the system board OVL is not permitted to alter the EISA nonvolatile memory.

OVL Memory Allocation

OVLs may find it useful to allocate dynamic storage space to hold configuration information. The following section of C code shows how the OVL memory support routines are used by an OVL. This example allocates memory for two nodes in a linked list. After the nodes have been linked, they are removed from the list and the allocated memory is released.

```
        .
        .
        .

/*
 *   Structure for linked list of memory entries
 */
typedef       struct Mem {
                    struct Mem      *next;
                    struct Mem      *rev;
                          int       nodeNumber:
              } MEM;

              .
              .
              .
              .
              .

MEM      *pHead;      /* Memory entries head pointer */
MEM      *pTail;      /* Memory entries tail pointer */
/*
 *   Initialize the memory entry nodes if
 *   the memory is allocated without errors.
 */
if(!(Support(ALLOCATE_MEMORY, sizeof(MEM), pHead))){
        if(!(Support(ALLOCATE_MEMORY, sizeof(MEM), &pTail))){
            /*
             *   Link the head node to the tail node.
             */
            pHead->next = pTail;
            pHead->prev = (MEM *)NULL;
            pHead->nodeNumber = 1;
            /*
             *   Link the tail node the head node.
             */
            pTail->next = (MEM *)NULL;
            pTail->prev = pHead;
            pTail->nodeNumber = 2;
                .
                .
```

```
                                   .
                                   .
                                   .

                    /*
                     *   Release the memory allocated
                     *   for the tail node.
                     */
                    Support(RELEASE_MEMORY, pTail);
            }
            /*
             *   Release the memory allocated
             *   for the head node.
             */
            Support(RELEASE_MEMORY, pHead);
     }

                                   .
                                   .
                                   .
```

OVL Summary

The OVL is one of the innovative features in the EISA configuration utility. Integrated with the execution of the utility, it provides a manufacturer with the means to customize the configuration process for an accessory card. OVLs can range from the simple OVL that selects configuration choices, to the full-blown system board OVL that oversees a variety of configuration activities.

```
/*  File:  OVL.H  */

#define FALSE                 0
#define TRUE                 ~FALSE
#define NULL                  0

#define FUNCTION_INIT         0
#define FUNCTION_CHANGE       1
#define FUNCTION_UPDATE       2

#define CHANGE_SELECTION      0    /* Called to edit a function choice.  */
#define CHANGE_RESULTS        1    /* Called if new choice is NOT ok.    */
#define CHANGE_SLOT           2    /* Informs OVL of slot change.        */
```

```
#define CHANGE_RESET               3     /* Reset choice to default value.    */
#define CHANGE_RESTORE             4     /* Reset choice to last saved value. */


#define UPDATE_CONFIGURATION       0     /* EISA CMOS has been written.        */
#define UPDATE_CHECK               1     /* Last chance to declare resources   */


#define TARGET_MACHINE             0x8000


#define REFRESH_VIDEO              0x8000 /* OVL wrote directly to screen. */
#define CANNOT_PROCESS_CARD        0x4000 /* OVL cannot handle this card.  */
#define MULTI_SUPPORT              0x2000 /* OVL can handle only one card. */
#define CONFIG_INCOMPLETE          0x1000 /* Cannot report all cfg text.   */


#define OVL_CHANGES_OK             0x0001 /* Utility accepted edit changes */
#define OVL_NO_CHANGES             0x0002 /* No changes made in edit panel */
#define OVL_OWNS_FUNCTION          0x0001 /* OVL will handle editing...    */
#define FREEFORM_DATA              0x0002 /* This data not cfg text data.  */


/* General support function equates */


#define ALLOCATE_MEMORY            0x0100 /* alloc some free memory       */
#define MODIFY_MEMORY              0x0101 /* adjust size of allocated mem */
#define RELEASE_MEMORY             0x0102 /* dispose of malloced memory   */


#define OPEN_PANEL                 0x0200 /* prepare a panel for display */
#define DISPLAY_PANEL              0x0201 /* display the panel           */
#define EDIT_PANEL                 0x0202 /* get panel mouse/keybd input */
#define CLOSE_PANEL                0x0204 /* close panel                 */


#define DIALOG_PANEL               1      /* panel for editing a choice  */
#define DEFAULT_STYLE              0      /* let utility pick panel style */
#define LIST_BOX                   11     /* field type for a list box   */
#define AUTO_PLACE                 -1     /* utility will ;locate panel  */

typedef
struct cfg_function {
        struct cfg_function   *next;
        unsigned char selections[26];     /* one byte/choice in cfg text */
        struct {
          unsigned  functionOwner : 1,    /* who owns editing of function */
                    functionType  : 1;    /* is function freeform data    */
        } flags;
```

```
        unsigned char  *choice;        /* text for current choice     */
        unsigned char  *subtype;
        unsigned char  *freeformData;
} CFG_FUNCTION;


typedef
struct {
        unsigned int        reserved00;
        unsigned int        slot;        /* what slot is the card in?  */
        char                *pcfgText;   /* cfg text for OVL functions */
        CFG_FUNCTION        *pcfgFunction; /* 1st OVL function         */
        unsigned long       reserved17[2];
} CFG_DATA;


typedef
struct ovl_parameters {

        unsigned char        subfunction;
        unsigned char        function;
        unsigned int         utilityVersion;
        unsigned int         ovlVersion;
        unsigned int         entryStatus;
        unsigned int         exitStatus;
        unsigned char        physicalSlotNumber;
        unsigned char        logicalSlotNumber;
        unsigned int         reserved10;
        unsigned char        eisaID[4];
        unsigned int         (far *Support)();
        unsigned long        memorySize;
        unsigned long        reserved1E;
        CFG_DATA        far *pcfgData;
        unsigned int         index;

} OVL_PARAMETERS;


typedef unsigned int PANEL;


typedef struct field {
        struct field *nextField;
        struct field *prevField;
        int fieldType;
        int rowFieldPrompt;
```

```
            int colFieldPrompt;
            int widFieldPrompt;
            unsigned char *promptText;
            int rowField;
            int colField;
            int widField;
            int lenField;
            union {
                    unsigned int  *lpInt;
                    unsigned char *lpStr;
            } fieldData;
            unsigned char *extendedFieldData;
            unsigned long  fieldOptions;
            unsigned char *fieldHelpText;
} PANEL_FIELD;

typedef struct group {
            struct group *nextGroup;
            struct group *prevGroup;
            unsigned char *groupText;
            int startingColumn;
            PANEL_FIELD *field;
}  PANEL_GROUP;

typedef struct {
            int eventID;
            PANEL_GROUP *selectedGroup;
            PANEL_FIELD *selectedField;
            unsigned int key;
            int mouse;
            int colMouse;
            int rowMouse
} EVENT;

typedef struct button {
            struct button *nextButton;
            struct button *prevButton;
            unsigned char *buttonText;
            unsigned int  buttonID;
            unsigned char *buttonHelpText;
            unsigned int  buttonFlags;
            unsigned int  quickKey;
} BUTTON;
```

```
typedef struct action {
        struct action *nextAction;
        struct action *prevAction;
        unsigned char *actionText;
        struct action *subAction;
        unsigned char *helpText;
        unsigned int  actionID;
        unsigned char actionFlags;
        unsigned int  quickKey;
} ACTION;
```

Summary

As shown in the examples in this chapter, the design of the EISA software is rather complex. However, by making all the configuration files and programs accessible to the programmer, the engineer, and the user, the EISA system provides power through versatility that is unequaled by any other technique. It is up to the user to select an easy, automatic system configuration or to become deeply involved in the details of the computer system.

The VGA Video Interface

This chapter provides general information on a typical VGA card. From it, you should be able to obtain a general understanding of a VGA system.

The subject of video, and particularly the VGA video interface as found on many EISA computers, is not a simple topic. As a result, concerned manufacturers such as Hewlett-Packard and Compaq have dedicated entire technical reference manuals to the topic of the video card. If you are doing any programming, you need to obtain the technical reference manual for that specific VGA card and determine the specific card BIOS and register characteristics.

VGA General Description

The VGA (Video Graphics Array) video interface is the most likely interface to be found on an EISA computer, although the EGA and various monochrome displays are also used. The VGA display is usually compatible with software written for the EGA (Enhanced Graphics Adapter) and with most software written for the CGA (Color Graphics Adapter) and the MDA (Monochrome Display Adapter). It also usually includes compatibility with much of the Hercules mode software. These compatibilities are usually provided through the use of additional programs supplied with the computer or VGA card to initialize the emulated mode. The VGA card must, however, be connected to an analog monitor. Such monitors are available in full color or monochrome versions depending on your requirements and budget. A ROM is usually included on the VGA card that provides a BIOS software interface for use in all display modes. The typical memory configuration is 256K configured as four 64K bit planes, though 512K of memory is also found on some VGA cards.

Compatibility Standards

There are two standards used to measure video compatibility. The first is compatibility to the BIOS level. This means that when you are writing programs that manipulate data on the screen, you will use the BIOS to do so. This level of compatibility is assured in virtually all of the VGA cards on the market. Software manufacturers who want to guarantee software compatibility write their software to this level of compatibility.

The second level of compatibility is to the register level. This is more difficult to assure, since there are a number of slightly different video cards available. Compatibility is usually maintained through an installation program that inserts the appropriate drivers into the program. This level of compatibility is required if the software you are using requires access to the VGA registers. This method decreases the time it takes to put information on the screen. While this is not so important in typical accounting or even word processing programs, CAD programs, graphics programs, games, and special video and animation programs quite often do use direct access to the registers of the VGA. Occasionally this results in some programs that are written for the VGA not always working on every system.

The VGA video interface consists of over 70 registers, divided into functional blocks. These functional blocks consist of the Sequencer, the CRT Controller, the Graphics Controller, the Attribute Controller, the Video DAC, and some miscellaneous registers.

VGA Video Connector

The VGA has a 15-pin connector that provides all the signals required for either a color or monochrome analog display. The pin connections for this connector are shown in Figure 7-1.

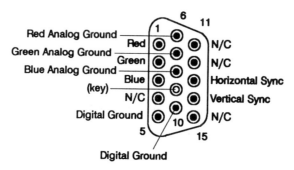

FIGURE 7-1   VGA Connector Pinout

Modes of Operation

The VGA card typically supports the modes shown in Table 7-1. Where a number is shown with a slash, such as 8/9, it means that either number is valid or supported in that mode, though it may be manufacturer dependent.

In addition to the modes in Table 7-1, some manufacturers have chosen to add and support a number of additional modes. These modes are not considered industry-standard compatible, though they may in time become very popular. They often deliver performance above and beyond the current standards, such as the Hercules mode that made significant contributions in monochrome graphics.

TABLE 7-1 Modes of Operation

Mode	Type	Colors	Alpha Size	Graphic Size
0/1	Alpha	16 of 256K	40x25	320/360x200/350/400
2/3	Alpha	16 of 256K	80x25	640/720x200/350/400
7	Alpha	Monochrome	80x25	720x350
4/5	Graphic	4 of 256K	40x25	320x200
6	Graphic	2 of 256K	80x25	640x200
8-C	n/a			
D	Graphic	16 of 256K	40x25	320x200
E	Graphic	16 of 256K	80x25	640x200
F	Graphic	- - -	-	640x350
10	Graphic	16 of 256K	80x25	640x350
11	Graphic	2 of 256K	80x30	640x480
12	Graphic	16 of 256K	80x30	640x480
13	Graphic	256 of 256K	40x25	320x200

VGA Components

The typical EISA VGA card consists of a small number of LSI (Large Scale Integration) components plus a few individual or discrete components. The LSI components provide the main functionality of the VGA card; the additional components provide additional external registers and signal drivers.

Sequencer	Creates the timing and control sequences on the VGA card. This includes timing for internal operations and access of the CPU.
CRT Controller	Synchronizes signals for the video signal which is output to the display. This includes programmable options such as timing and polarity, and most display-related characteristics.
Graphics Controller	Provides formatting for the data in the various modes.
Attribute Controller	Provides control over the color palette and character attributes.

Programming the VGA

Direct programming of the VGA is not recommended since it can result in incompatibility when the program is moved to machines with a different VGA card. However, there are times when direct programming is desirable, such as when speed is important for real time animation (CAD programs or games). In this case, different drivers will have to be provided for each of the possible VGA cards that might be used.

Register Definitions

The following pages show the contents and provide general information on the registers found in a typical VGA card and which you can use to get a general understanding of the registers in a VGA system. It represents only those registers that *should* be found in all VGA cards. If you are doing any programming for a specific VGA card or application, you will need to obtain the technical reference manual for that specific VGA card and determine the exact register characteristics.

The information presented represents data that is common to both EISA computer manufacturers, such as Hewlett-Packard and Compaq, and other non-EISA computers that also use the VGA standard, such as IBM.

External Registers

Miscellaneous Output Register   The miscellaneous output register is a write-only register located at address 3C2h.

Bit	Function
D0	Selects the I/O addresses for the monochrome or color mode.
=0	Sets the CRT Controller to 3B*x*h and the Input Status register 1 to 3BAh (monochrome mode).
=1	Sets the CRT Controller to 3D*x*h and the Input Status register 1 to 3DAh (color mode).
D1	
=0	Video RAM is disabled from the CPU.
=1	Video RAM responds at the address set by the Control Data Select register of the graphics controller.
D3,D2	
=0,=0	Selects 25.175 MHz clock.
=0,=1	Selects 28.322 MHz clock.
=1,=0	Selects external clock.
=1,=1	Reserved.
D4	Labeled as reserved by most application programs.
D5	
=0	Low page (64K) of memory is selected.
=1	High page of memory is selected.

D6

=0   Horizontal retrace polarity is positive.

=1   Horizontal retrace polarity is negative.

D7

=0   Vertical retrace polarity is positive.

=1   Vertical retrace polarity is negative.

Feature Control Register   The Feature Control register is a carry-over from the EGA cards and is not implemented on some VGA cards. If you need these functions, refer to the technical reference manual for your VGA card.

Input Status Register 0   The Input Status register 0 is also a carry-over from the EGA cards. In EISA computers there are, typically, no switches used to set the card configuration. Therefore, this function may or may not be implemented in your particular card. As in the Feature Control register, if you require this information in your programs you will have to refer to the technical reference manual for your VGA.

Bit	Function
D0-D3	Not used.
D4	In IBM computers, allows the CPU to determine the type of display attached to the system but may not be required in an EISA system.
D5,D6	Not used.

D7

=0   Vertical retrace interrupt is cleared.

=1   Vertical retrace interrupt is pending.

Input Status Register 1   The Input Status register 1 is a read-only register located at port address 3DAh.

Bit	Function
D0	
=0	Raster is not in a retrace interval and screen updates should be inhibited.
=1	Raster is in a vertical or horizontal retrace interval.
D1,D2	Used for light pen information in EGA cards and not implemented in many VGA cards.
D3	
=0	Video information is being displayed.
=1	Card is in a vertical retrace interval.
D4,D5	Connected to the attribute controller and select two of the eight color outputs of the attribute controller.
D6,D7	Not used.

Sequencer Registers

Sequencer Address Register   The Sequence Address register points to other internal registers of the graphics controller (the Sequencer Address index). These bits determine the register to be accessed in the next register access.

Bit	Function
D0-D2	Sequencer address index.
D3-D7	Bits D3-D7 are not used.

Reset Register   The Reset register is a write-only register pointed to by a value of 00h in the Sequencer Address register.

Bit	Function
D0	
=0	Causes the sequencer to clear asynchronously and halt.
=1	Causes the sequencer to run unless D1=0.
D1	
=0	Causes the sequencer to clear synchronously and halt.
=1	Causes the sequencer to run unless D0 is cleared.

D2-D7   Not used.

Clocking Mode Register   The Clocking Mode register is a write-only register pointed to by a value of 01h in the Sequencer Address register.

Bit   **Function**

D0

=0   Causes the sequencer to generate character clocks that are 9 dots wide.

=1   Causes the sequencer to generate character clocks that are 8 dots wide.

D1   Not used.

D2

=0   Causes the display serializers in the graphics controller to be reloaded every character clock.

=1   Causes the display serializers in the graphics controller to be reloaded every other character clock.

D3

=0   Selects the sequencer master clock input to be output on the dot clock output pin.

=1   Causes the master clock to be divided by 2 to generate the dot clock.

D4

=0   Causes the video serializers to be loaded every character clock.

=1   Causes the video serializers to be loaded every fourth clock cycle.

D5

=0   Selects normal screen operation.

=1   Turns off the video screen.

D6,D7   Not used.

Map Mask Register   The Map Mask Register is a write-only register pointed to by a value of 02h in the Sequencer Address register. The Map Mask register enables the maps as follows:

Bit	Function
D0	
=1	Map 0 is enabled.
=0	Map 0 is disabled.
D1	
=1	Map 0 is enabled.
=0	Map 0 is disabled.
D2	
=1	Map 0 is enabled.
=0	Map 0 is disabled.
D3	
=1	Map 0 is enabled.
=0	Map 0 is disabled.
D4-D7	Not used.

Character Map Select Register   The Character Map Select register is a write-only register pointed to by a value of 03h in the Sequencer Address register.

Bit	Function
D1/D0	Select the plane that generates alpha characters when attribute bit 3 is 0 according to the following:

D1	D0	Map	Location
0	0	0	1st 8K of Plane 2 Bank 0
0	1	1	2nd 8K of Plane 2 Bank 1
1	0	2	3rd 8K of Plane 2 Bank 2
1	1	3	4th 8K of Plane 2 Bank 3

D3/D2   Character Map Select A: select the plane that generates alpha characters when attribute bit 3 is 1 according to the following:

D3	D2	Map	Location
0	0	0	1st 8K of Plane 2 Bank 0
0	1	1	2nd 8K of Plane 2 Bank 1
1	0	2	3rd 8K of Plane 2 Bank 2
1	1	3	4th 8K of Plane 2 Bank 3

Memory Mode Register   The Memory Mode register is a write-only register pointed to by a value of 04h in the Sequencer Address register.

Bit	Function
D0	Reserved.
D1	
=1	More than 256K of display memory is present. This bit must be set to enable character map selection.
D2	
=0	Directs even CPU addresses to access maps 0 and 2 while odd CPU addresses access maps 1 and 3.
=1	Causes CPU addresses to access data sequentially within a map.

CRT Controller Registers

Address Register   The Address register points to the internal registers of the CRT controller. These bits determine which register will be pointed to in the next register-write operation.

Bit	Function
D0-D4	CRT Controller Register index.
D5-D7	Not used.

Horizontal Total Register The Horizontal Total register is a write-only register pointed to by a value of 00h in the CRT Controller Address register. It specifies the number of characters in a horizontal scan line. The value in the register is the total number of characters on the scan line minus 5.

Horizontal Display Enable End Register The Horizontal Display Enable End register is a write-only register pointed to by a value of 01h in the CRT Controller Address register. It defines the total number of displayed characters in a horizontal line. The value in the register is the total number of characters on the scan line minus 1.

Start Horizontal Blanking Register The Start Horizontal Blanking register is a write-only register pointed to by a value of 02h in the CRT Controller Address register. The contents of this register define the time when the horizontal blanking will start.

End Horizontal Blanking Register The End Horizontal Blanking register is a write-only register pointed to by a value of 03h in the CRT Controller Address register. The contents of this register define the time when the horizontal blanking will end.

Bit	Function
D0-D4	Define the blanking signal width. This is equal to the value of the Start Blanking Register plus the width of the blanking signal in character clock cycles. These five bits will contain the five least significant bits; the most significant bit is bit 7 of the End Horizontal Retrace Register.
D6/D5	Define skew, as shown below:

D6	D5	Skew
0	0	0
0	1	1

1	0	2
1	1	3

D7   Not used but must be set to 1.

Start Horizontal Retrace Pulse Register   The Start Horizontal Retrace Pulse register is a write-only register pointed to by a value of 04h in the CRT Controller Address register. It defines the character position where the horizontal retrace pulse becomes active.

End Horizontal Retrace Pulse Register   The end Horizontal Retrace Pulse register is a write-only register pointed to by a value of 05h in the CRT Controller Address register. It defines the character count where the horizontal retrace pulse becomes inactive.

Bit	Function
D0-D4	Define the horizontal retrace skew.
D6/D5	Define skew, as shown below:

D6	**D5**	**Skew**
0	0	0
0	1	1
1	0	2
1	1	3

D7   Not used but must be set to 1.

Vertical Total Register   The Vertical Total register is a write-only register pointed to by a value of 06h in the CRT Controller Address register. It defines the number of horizontal raster scans on the CRT screen, including the vertical retrace.

CRT Controller Overflow Register   The CRT Controller Overflow register is a write-only register pointed to by a value of 07h in the CRT Controller Address register. It contains the eighth or ninth bit of the other control registers where required.

Bit	Content
D0	Bit 8 of the Vertical Total register
D1	Bit 8 of the Vertical Display Enable End register
D2	Bit 8 of the Vertical Retrace register
D3	Bit 8 of the Start Vertical Blank register
D4	Bit 8 of the Line Compare register
D5	Bit 8 of the Vertical Total register
D6	Bit 9 of the Vertical Display Enable End register
D7	Bit 9 of the Vertical Retrace register

Preset Row Scan Register   The Preset Row Scan register is a write-only register pointed to by a value of 08h in the CRT Controller Address register.

Bit	Function
D0-D4	Specify the starting row scan count after a vertical retrace.
D5,D6	Control byte-panning modes as required for PEL panning operations.
D7	Not used.

Maximum Scan Line Register   The Maximum Scan Line register is a write-only register pointed to by a value of 09h in the CRT Controller Address register.

Bit	Function
D0-D4	Specify the number of scan lines per character row, minus one.
D5	Contains bit 9 of the Start Vertical Blank register.
D6	Contains bit 9 of the Line Compare register.
D7	
=1	Causes a 200- to 400-line conversion, displaying each line twice.
=0	Provides normal display.

Cursor Start Register   The Cursor Start register is a write-only register pointed to by a value of 0Ah in the CRT Controller Address register.

Bit	Function
D0-D4	Specify the row scan of a character line where a cursor is to begin.
D5	
=0	Turns the cursor on.
=1	turns the cursor off.
D6,D7	Not used.

Cursor End Register   The Cursor End register is a write-only register pointed to by a value of 0Bh in the CRT Controller Address register. It specifies the row scan of a character line where a cursor is to end.

Bit	Function
D0-D4	Define the row scan where the cursor is to end.
D6/D5	Define skew, as shown below:

D6	**D5**	**Skew**
0	0	Zero character skew
0	1	One character skew
1	0	Two character skew
1	1	Three character skew

Bit	Function
D7	Not used.

Start Address High Register   The Start Address High register is a read/write register pointed to by a value of 0Ch in the CRT Controller Address register. It specifies the first address, after a vertical retrace, where the display on the screen begins. This register contains the 8 high-order bits of the address.

Start Address Low Register   The Start Address Low register is a read/write register pointed to by a value of 0Dh in the

CRT Controller Address register. It specifies the first address, after a vertical retrace, where the display on the screen begins. This register contains the 8 low-order bits of the address.

Cursor Location High Register   The Cursor Location High register is a read/write register pointed to by a value of 0Eh in the CRT Controller Address register. It specifies the start address for the cursor. This register contains the 8 high-order bits of the address.

Cursor Location Low Register   The Cursor Location Low register is a read/write register pointed to by a value of 0Fh in the CRT Controller Address register. It specifies the start address for the cursor. This register contains the 8 low-order bits of the address.

Vertical Retrace Start Register   The Vertical Retrace Start register is a write-only register pointed to by a value of 10h in the CRT Controller Address register. It defines the position of the vertical retrace start signal.

Vertical Retrace End Register   The Vertical Retrace End register is a write-only register pointed to by a value of 11h in the CRT Controller Address register.

Bit	Function
D0-D3	Specify the horizontal scan line count length.
D4	
=0	Clears the vertical interrupt generated on the CRTINT output of the CRT controller.
=1	This bit is set to 1 so that the flip-flop does not hold the interrupts inactive.
D5	
=0	Enables the vertical interrupt of the CRT Controller.
=1	Disables the vertical retrace interrupt.

D6

=1   Generates 5 refresh cycles per horizontal line.

=0   Generates 3 refresh cycles per horizontal line.

D7

=0   Enables writing to R0-7.

=1   Disables writing to R0-7.

Vertical Display Enable End Register   The Vertical
Display Enable End register is a write-only register pointed to by
a value of 12h in the CRT Controller Address register. It defines
8 bits of the address that specifies the scan line position where the
screen display ends.

Offset Register   The Offset register is a write-only register pointed to by a value of 13h in the CRT Controller Address
register. It defines the logical line width of the screen.

Underline Location Register   The Underline Location
register is a write-only register pointed to by a value of 14h in the
CRT Controller Address register.

Bit	Function
D0-D4	Specify the horizontal row scan count where the under-line will occur.
D5	
=0	Causes the memory address pointer to be clocked with the character clock, divided by 2.
=1	Causes the memory address pointer to be clocked with the character clock, divided by 4.
D6	
=0	Gives control to the CRTC Mode Control Register, bit 6.
=1	Causes the memory addresses to be doubleword ad-dresses.
D7	Not used.

Start Vertical Blanking Register The Start Vertical Blanking register is a write-only register pointed to by a value of 15h in the CRT Controller Address register. It contains the low-order 8 bits of the horizontal scan line count where the vertical blanking pulse becomes active.

End Vertical Blanking Register The End Vertical Blanking register is a write-only register pointed to by a value of 16h in the CRT Controller Address register. It specifies the horizontal scan line count where the vertical blanking pulse becomes inactive.

Mode Control Register The Mode Control register is a write-only register pointed to by a value of 17h in the CRT Controller Address register.

Bit	Function
D0	
=0	Substitutes the row scan address bit 0 for memory address bit 13 during active display time.
=1	No substitution takes place.
D1	
=0	Substitutes the row scan counter bit 1 for memory bit address bit 14 during active display time.
=1	No substitution takes place.
D2	
=0	Selects the horizontal retrace clock.
=1	Selects the horizontal retrace clock divided by 2.
D3	
=0	Memory address counter is clocked by the character clock input.
=1	Memory address is clocked by the character clock input divided by 2.
D4	Not used.

D5

=0   Selects memory address counter bit MA13.

=1   Selects MA15.

D6

=0   Selects word mode.

=1   Selects the byte mode.

D7

=0   Clears vertical and horizontal retraces.

=1   Enables the vertical and horizontal retraces.

Line Compare Register   The Line Compare register is a write-only register pointed to by a value of 18h in the CRT Controller Address register. It implements a split screen function.

Graphics Controller Registers

Graphics Address Register   The Graphics Address register is a write-only register located at port address 3CEh. It points to other internal registers of the graphics controller. The 4 least-significant bits determine the register pointed to in the next register-write operation.

Bit	Function
D0-D3	Point to the control registers.
D4-D7	Not used.

Set/Reset Register   The Set/Reset register is a write-only register pointed to by a value of 00h in the Graphics Address register.

Bit	Function
D0-D3	Enable the set/reset function of the four memory maps.
D4-D7	Not used.

Enable Set/Reset Register   The Enable Set/Reset register is a write-only register pointed to by the value of 01h in the Graphics Address register.

Bit	Function
D0-D3	Enable the set/reset function in conjunction with the Set/Reset register.
D4-D7	Not used.

Color Compare Register   The Color Compare register is a write-only register pointed to by a value of 02h in the Graphics Address register.

Bit	Function
D0-D3	Content is compared to the data read from display memory maps 0 to 3 *if* the Mode register has the read mode set.
D4-D7	Not used.

Data Rotate Register   The Data Rotate register is a write-only register pointed to by a value of 03h in the Graphics Address register.

Bit	Function
D0-D2	Binary encoded value representing the rotate count.
D3-D4	Operate as follows:

D4	D3	Operation
0	0	No change
0	1	Logical 'AND' between Data and latched data
1	0	Logical 'OR' between Data and latched data
1	1	Logical 'XOR' between Data and latched data

D5-D7	Not used.

Read Map Select Register   The Read Map Select register is a write-only register pointed to by a value of 04h in the Graphics Address register.

Bit	Function
D1/D0	Select the memory map from which the CPU reads data.

D1	D0	
0	0	Map 0
0	1	Map 1
1	0	Map 2
1	1	Map 3

Bit	Function
D2-D7	Not used.

Mode Register   The Mode register is a write-only register pointed to by a value of 05h in the Graphics Address register.

Bit	Function
D0,D1	Select the write mode.
D2	Not used.
D3	
=0	Causes the CPU to read the data from the display memory planes.
=1	Causes the CPU to read the result of the logical comparison between the 4 display memory planes data and the contents of the Color Compare register.
D4	
=1	Puts the graphics controller in the odd/even addressing mode.
D5	
=0	Formats the serial data stream for normal or high resolution operation.
=1	Defines the operation of the graphics section shift registers. In mode 4 and 5 (low resolution 320x200) a 1 formats the serial data stream with even bits on even-numbered maps and odd bits on odd-numbered maps.

D6

=0   Allows bit D5 to control loading of the shift registers.

=1   Causes the registers to be loaded in 256 color mode.

D7   Not used.

    Miscellaneous Register   The Miscellaneous register is a write-only register pointed to by a value of 06h in the Graphics Address register.

Bit	Function
D0	

=1   Selects the graphics mode. This disables the character generator latches. The bit D0 is output on the GRAPHICS pin of the controller.

D1

=1   Replaces the CPU address bit A0 with a higher order address bit.

D2-D3   Control the mapping of the address memory buffers into the CPU address space:

D3	D2	
0	0	A000h for 128K
0	1	A000h for 64K
1	0	B000h for 32K
1	1	B800h for 32K

D4-D7   Not used.

    Color Don't Care Register   The Color Don't Care register is a write-only register pointed to by a value of 07h in the Graphics Address register.

Bit	Function
D0	

=0   Color plane 0 is not tested.

D1

=0   Color plane 1 is not tested.

D2

=0   Color plane 2 is not tested.

D3

=0   Color plane 3 is not tested.

D4-D7   Not used.

Bit Mask Register   The Bit Mask register is a write-only register pointed to by a value of 08h in the Graphics Address register. Any bit programmed to 0 in this register will cause the corresponding bit in each of the four memory planes to be immune to change.

Attribute Controller Registers

Attribute Address Register   The Attribute Address register is a 6-bit write-only register that points to other internal registers of the attribute controller.

Bit   **Function**

D0-D4   Attribute address bits.

D5

=0   Allows loading of the Color Palette registers.

=1   Allows normal operation by enabling access to the Color Palette registers for CRT read operations.

D6,D7   Not used.

Palette Registers   Palette registers are sixteen 6-bit write-only registers pointed to when the contents of the Address register is 00h through 0Fh. These registers allow a mapping between the text attribute or graphic color input and the display color on the CRT screen. The six bits, D0 through D5, are P0 through P5 respectively. D6 and D7 are not used.

Mode Control Register   The Mode Control register is a write-only register pointed to when the contents of the Address register is 10h.

Bit	Function
D0	
=0	Selects alphanumeric mode.
=1	Selects graphics mode.
D1	
=0	Selects color display attributes.
=1	Selects monochrome display attributes.
D2	
=0	Makes the ninth dot the same as the background.
=1	Enables the special line graphics character codes for the monochrome display adapter.
D3	
=0	Selects the background intensity for the attribute input.
=1	Enables the blink attribute in alphanumeric and graphics modes.
D4	Not used.
D5	
=0	Causes a line compare to have no effect on the output of the PEL Panning register.
=1	Forces the output of the PEL Panning register to 0 after a successful compare in the CRT controller.
D6	
=1	Causes 8 bits to be available to select a color in mode 13h. Otherwise, this bit should be off.
D7	Selects the source for the P4 and P5 video bits.
=0	Source is the outputs of the Palette registers.
=1	Source is the Color Select register.

Overscan Color Register   The Overscan Color register is a write-only register pointed to when the contents of the address register is 11h. It defines the overscan or border color displayed on the CRT screen. Bits 0-7 correspond to P0-7, respectively.

Color Plane Enable Register   The Color Plane Enable register is a write-only register pointed to when the contents of the Address register is 12h.

Bit	Function
D0-D3	A 1 in any of the bits D0-D3 enables the respective display memory color plane 0-3.
D4-D5	Selects the color outputs which are input to the Input Status Register 1. The values of these bits will vary among manufacturers.
D6,D7	Not used.

Horizontal Pel Panning Register   The Horizontal Pel Panning register is a write-only register pointed to when the contents of the Address register is 13h.

Bit	Function
D0-D3	Select the number of pixels to shift the display data to the left.
D4-D7	Not used.

Color Select Register   The Color Select is a read/write register pointed to when the contents of the Address register is 14h.

Bit	Function
D0,D1	Can be used instead of the P4 and P5 bits from the Attribute Palette register.
D2,D3	Two high-order bits of the 8-bit digital color value.
D4-D7	Not used.

Using VGA BIOS Functions

The VGA card usually contains an IBM-compatible ROM BIOS that provides support for the VGA hardware. This includes fonts for text and graphics modes, and power-on tests to assure that the hardware is functioning properly.

The VGA BIOS-supported modes can be divided into two types, alpha (Alphanumeric or A/N) and graphics (also called APA or All Points Addressable). Some of the following functions apply to only one of these types, while others expect different parameters based on whether the current display type is alpha or graphics.

The VGA BIOS functions are accessed using interrupt 10H. The function code is placed in register AH, and other information is placed in the corresponding registers as indicated. Where no exit values are given, none are present. The following functions are usually present in all implementations of the VGA BIOS. Some implementations may provide additional functions. Refer to your technical reference manual to determine if you have any additional functions.

Set Mode

Usually you need to tell the VGA what mode to use. This is done with a Set Mode function in the BIOS.

```
Entry:      AL = mode
            AH = 00h
```

The Set Mode function sets the system to a text mode or a graphics mode as discussed in the "Modes of Operation" section of this chapter.

Get Video State

You might also need to determine the mode to which the VGA BIOS is set. This is done with the Get Video State function.

```
Entry:      AH = 0Fh

Exit:       AL = mode currently set
            AH = number of character columns on screen
            BH = current active display page
```

Set Active Page

The VGA contains 256K to 512K of memory, of which only a small amount is used at any time. Most display modes have several pages or screens that can be displayed, though only one screen can be active at a time. The other screens are accessible by the CPU but are not displayed on the screen.

```
Entry:      AL = new page value
            AH = 05h
```

Note that the VGA BIOS maintains the current cursor position for each page.

Set Cursor Type

The cursor shows where the next character will be placed on the screen. The shape of the cursor can be set using the Set Cursor Type function as shown:

```
Entry:      AH = 01h
            CH = start line for cursor (bits 4-0)
            CL = end line for cursor (bits 4-0)
```

The shape of the cursor can be defined as anything between a blinking box and one line.

Set Cursor Position

Through the BIOS, all characters written to the screen are placed at the current cursor position. The program must specify where the cursor is placed.

```
Entry:        AH = 02h
              DH = row
              DL = column
              BH = page number
```

Read Cursor Position

When the cursor position is set, all character reads and writes will be to that position. If you need to determine the cursor position use the Read Cursor Position function:

```
Entry:        BH = page number
              AH = 03h

Exit:         DH = row
              DL = column
              CX = current cursor type
```

Write Text Functions

Once a cursor position is known, you can place text at that position. There are several ways to do this as shown in the following sections.

Write Character and Attribute   The Write Character and Attribute function allows you to write both the specified character and its attribute, such as color and intensity. The attribute information is shown in Table 7-2 following the function parameter information.

```
Entry:        BH = page
              CX = number of times to write character
              AL = character to write
              BL = attribute of character (Alpha mode)
              BL = color of character (Graphics mode)
              AH = 09h
```

In graphics mode, if bit 7 of BL is 1, then the color is XORed with the screen.

Write Character Only Function   The Write Character Only function is the same as the Write Character and Attribute

TABLE 7-2 Character Attributes

Attribute	I	R	G	B	Monochrome	Color
00h	0	0	0	0	Black	Black
01h	0	0	0	1	Underline	Blue
02h	0	0	1	0	Video	Green
03h	0	0	1	1	Video	Cyan
04h	0	1	0	0	Video	Red
05h	0	1	0	1	Video	Magenta
06h	0	1	1	0	Video	Brown
07h	0	1	1	1	Video	White
08h	1	0	0	0	Black	Dark Gray
09h	1	0	0	1	Underline	Light Blue
0Ah	1	0	1	0	Video	Light Green
0Bh	1	0	1	1	Video	Light Cyan
0Ch	1	1	0	0	Video	Light Red
0Dh	1	1	0	1	Video	Light Magenta
0Eh	1	1	1	0	Video	Yellow
0Fh	1	1	1	1	Video	Intensified White

function above, except that it does not alter the attribute information for the character.

```
Entry:    BH = page
          BL = foreground color (Graphics only)
          CX = count of characters to write
          AL = character to write
          AH = 0Ah
```

Read Character and Attribute Function   The Read Character and Attribute function returns the character and associated attribute at the cursor position.

```
Entry:      AH = 08h
            BH = page

Exit:       AL = character read
            AH = attribute of character read (Alpha modes only)
```

Write TTY Function   The Write TTY function writes a character to the screen and then moves the cursor to the right. As the cursor goes to the right side of the screen, it will wrap back to the left and down one line as if receiving a CR and LF. If the cursor goes off the bottom of the screen, it will automatically scroll up the screen one line.

```
Entry:      AH = 0Eh
            AL = character to write
            BL = foreground color in graphics mode
```

The Write TTY function has several predefined special characters which perform special action:

- CR returns the cursor to column 0 on the same line.
- LF leaves the column position the same but goes down one line, scrolling the screen if the cursor is at the bottom of the screen.
- BS moves the cursor position back one position.
- Bell outputs a tone to the speaker.

Write String Function   The Write String function allows writing more than one character at a time to the screen. It also allows writing one attribute for the whole screen or a character and an attribute for each position on the screen, so each character has its own attribute. It can also update the cursor position or leave it where it started.

```
Entry:      AH = 13h
            ES:BP = pointer to string
            CX = character only count
            DX = position to begin string
            BH = page number
```

AL = 0:   Fixed attribute, cursor not moved
             BL = attribute

AL = 1:   Fixed attribute, cursor moved
             BL = attribute

AL = 2:   String includes attributes, cursor not moved

AL = 3:   String includes attributes, cursor moved

This function responds to the CR, LF, BS and Bell codes in a manner similar to the Write TTY function.

Scroll Up

The Scroll Up function scrolls the screen up a set number of lines.

```
Entry:    AH = 06h
          AL = number of lines (0 = entire window)
          CH,CL = row, column of upper left corner of scroll
          DH,DL = row, column of lower right corner of scroll
          BH = attribute used on blank line or area
```

Scroll Down

The Scroll Down function scrolls the screen down a set number of lines.

```
Entry:    AH = 07h
          AL = number of lines (0 means entire window)
          CH,CL = row, column of upper left corner of scroll
          DH,DL = row, column of lower right corner of scroll
          BH  = attribute to be used on blank line
```

Specifying 0 lines to be scrolled will clear the defined window.

Read Dot Function

The Read Dot function returns the color value of the specified pixel.

```
Entry:      AH = 0Dh
            BH = page
            DX = row number
            CX = column number


Exit:       AL = color of dot read
```

Write Dot Function

The Write Dot function writes a color to a specified pixel.

```
Entry:      AH = 0Ch
            BH = page
            DX = row number
            CX = column number
            AL = color value
```

Set Color Palette Function

The Set Color Palette function allows the programmer to define different colors to be displayed on the screen.

```
Entry:      AH = 0Bh
            BH = palette color ID being set
            BL = color value to be used with that color ID

   Where:   Color ID = 0 selects the background color
            Color ID = 1 selects the palette to be used:
                      0 = Green(1)/Red(2)/Brown(3)
                      1 = Cyan(1)/Magenta(2)/White(3)
```

Note that there are several different implementations of this function. You should verify your implementation with the technical reference manual for your system to assure compatibility. In general, this function provides compatibility with the CGA BIOS code.

Programming Examples

Display a Character Using MS-DOS

```
;
;   The following assembly language program uses the MS-DOS
;   operating system to display a character on the screen.
;   This program can be assembled, linked, and run
;   from MS-DOS.
;

_TEXT         SEGMENT BYTE PUBLIC 'CODE'
_TEXT         ENDS


_DATA         SEGMENT WORD PUBLIC 'DATA'
_DATA         ENDS



_TEXT         SEGMENT
              ASSUME      CS:_TEXT


              ;
              ; Display "A" to standard output.
              ;
              mov         dl,"A"          ;Set the character to output
              mov         ah,02h          ;Set the character output function
              int         21h             ;Invoke DOS to display the character


              ;
              ; Exit back to DOS.
              ;
              mov         ax,4C00h
              int         21h

_TEXT         ENDS
              END
```

Display a Character String Using MS-DOS

```
;
;   The following program uses the MS-DOS operating system to display a
```

```
;   string of characters on the screen.  This program can be
;   assembled, linked, and run from MS-DOS.
;

_TEXT          SEGMENT BYTE PUBLIC 'CODE'
_TEXT          ENDS


_DATA          SEGMENT WORD PUBLIC 'DATA'
_DATA          ENDS


LF             EQU            0Ah              ;Line feed
CR             EQU            0Dh              ;Carriage return



_DATA          SEGMENT

GoodbyeStringDB 'Good-bye',CR,LF,'$' ;'$' terminated Good-bye string

_DATA          ENDS



_TEXT          SEGMENT
               ASSUME         CS:_TEXT

               mov            ax,_DATA
               mov            ds,ax
               ASSUME         ds:_DATA

               ;
               ; Display "Good-bye" to the standard output and move the
               ; display cursor to a new line.
               ;
               mov            dx,OFFSET GoodbyeString    ;Set string address

               mov            ah,09h        ;Set the string output function
               int            21h           ;Invoke DOS to display the string

               ;
               ; Exit back to DOS.
               ;
```

```
          mov              ax,4C00h
          int              21h


_TEXT     ENDS
          END
```

Display a Character Using BIOS

```
;
; The following assembly language program uses the BIOS to
; display a character on the screen.  This program can be
; assembled, linked, and run from MS-DOS.
;


_TEXT     SEGMENT BYTE PUBLIC 'CODE'
_TEXT     ENDS


_DATA     SEGMENT WORD PUBLIC 'DATA'
_DATA     ENDS



_TEXT     SEGMENT
          ASSUME         CS:_TEXT


          ;
          ; Display "A" to the screen.
          ;
          mov            al,"A"
          mov            ah,0Eh         ;Set BIOS write character function


          int            10h            ;Invoke BIOS to display the character


          ;
          ; Exit back to DOS.
          ;
          mov            ax,4C00h
          int            21h


_TEXT     ENDS
          END
```

Display a Character String Using BIOS

```
;
;  The following program uses the BIOS to display a string
;  of characters on the screen.  This program can be assembled,
;  linked, and run from MS-DOS.
;

_TEXT          SEGMENT BYTE PUBLIC 'CODE'
_TEXT          ENDS


_DATA          SEGMENT WORD PUBLIC 'DATA'
_DATA          ENDS


CR             EQU          0Dh           ;Carriage return
LF             EQU          0Ah           ;Line feed



_DATA          SEGMENT

GoodbyeStringDB 'Good-bye',0     ;NULL terminated Good-bye string


_DATA          ENDS



_TEXT          SEGMENT
               ASSUME       CS:_TEXT

               mov          ax,_DATA
               mov          ds,ax
               ASSUME       ds:_DATA



               ;
               ; Display "Good bye" to the screen and move the
               ; display cursor to a new line.
               ;
               mov          si,OFFSET GoodbyeString   ;Set string address

string_10:
               lodsb                                  ;Get the next string character
               or           al,al
```

```
            jz          string_20          ;End of string?

       mov         ah,0Eh             ;Set BIOS write character function
       int         10h                ;Invoke BIOS to Display character

       jmp         string_10          ;Check for more characters

string_20:

       mov         al,CR              ;Set carriage return
       mov         ah,0Eh             ;Set BIOS write character function
       int         10h                ;Invoke BIOS to Display character

       mov         al,LF              ;Set line feed
       mov         ah,0Eh             ;Set BIOS write character function
       int         10h                ;Invoke BIOS to Display character

       ;
       ; Exit back to DOS.
       ;
       mov         ax,4C00h
       int         21h

_TEXT  ENDS
       END
```

Summary

Most of the EISA computers use the VGA video standard. This standard allows a nominal display resolution of 640 x 480 pixels and an ultra-high resolution of up to 1024 x 768 pixels. In spite of these high resolutions, some applications are able to handle only the lower resolutions of CGA or monochrome modes. The VGA cards planned for the EISA machines are fully compatible with the earlier software modes, so no software problems should be encountered when upgrading to an EISA machine.

CHAPTER
8

Serial Data
Communications

This chapter covers the serial ports (RS232 interface) found on a typical EISA computer system. The RS232 interface is used to connect modems, printers, or terminals (in multi-user systems) to the computer, and sometimes to connect one computer with another for high-speed transfer of files between two computers.

First, to eliminate one misconception, the EIA RS232 interface specification does not define any type of data format. It does not require 7 or 8 data bits, or require ASCII or Baudot code. The specification that defines the RS232 interface defines only the signals which should appear on the connector. However, since the two are so closely related, serial data formats are also covered in this chapter.

In addition, the RS232 interface specification does not define many of the signals now appearing on the connector. Many manufacturers reassign some of the pins for their own use, thus rendering the standard somewhat ineffective.

Another complicating factor is that the function of the pins depends on whether the computer or peripheral uses a DCE (Data Communications Equipment) or a DTE (Data Terminal Equipment) configuration. DCE configuration is that typically found on a modem, and DTE configuration is that typically found on a terminal. The computer itself may be either configuration, but usually is DTE. This configuration (DCE or DTE) determines whether the connector is expecting to send or receive a given signal on a specified pin. We'll get into this in more depth later on in the chapter, since it is a source of much confusion for many computer professionals.

Computer sales people, consultants, and users are frequently puzzled over the interconnections between the computer, the printer, the modem, and other terminals. Each computer manufacturer may incorporate variations from the EIA RS-232 standard, though the EISA computers will typically be more uniform and conform to what is presented here. Therefore, the object of this chapter is to help you understand which signals the computer and peripherals are expecting, on which connector pin, and how to make the computer match the peripheral device.

Because of the deviations from the specification standard, this book cannot hope to be 100% accurate in all applications. What is presented here is the information you need to understand your

RS232 serial interface and help resolve problems you may have with it.

The Serial Connector

The serial port connector is normally a 9-pin or a 25-pin D-type connector. Looking at the connector as it appears on the equipment, the pins are numbered as shown in Figures 8-1 and 8-2. Note that the pin numbering will be a mirror image as you look at the cable end, although the numbers on the connectors will match.

In a 25-pin installation, such as is found on earlier personal computers and on some port expansion cards, the female connector is mounted on the computer equipment and the male connector is mounted on the serial interface cable. This means that a cable used

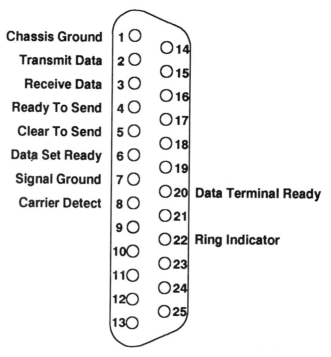

FIGURE 8-1   Typical 25-pin RS232 Connector Pin Numbering

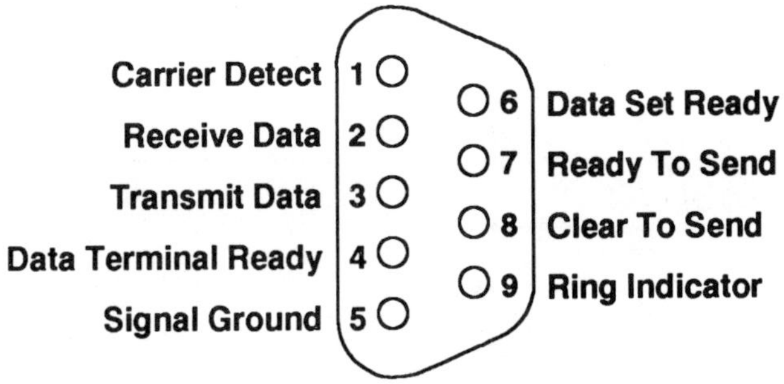

FIGURE 8-2   Typical 9-pin RS232 Connector Pin Numbering

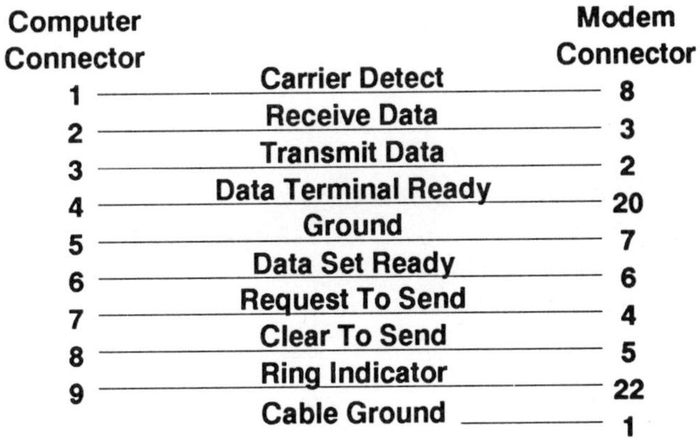

FIGURE 8-3   Wiring of a Typical Modem 9- to 25-pin RS232 Cable

to connect two pieces of equipment, such as a computer and a modem or printer, will have a male connector at both ends.

In a normal 9-pin installation, such as is found on most EISA computers, a 9-pin male connector is mounted on the computer and a female connector is mounted on the serial interface cable, but only on the computer end of the cable. On the peripheral end, such as a modem or printer, the cable will probably have a 25-pin male connector and the modem or printer will have a female connector. Wiring for typical cables for a modem and a printer is shown schematically in Figures 8-3 and 8-4.

```
Computer                                      Printer
Connector                                     Connector
    1 ——————— Carrier Detect ———————— 4
    2 ——————— Receive Data ——————————— 2
    3 ——————— Transmit Data ——————————— 3
    4 ——————— Data Terminal Ready ————— 5
                                          └—— 6
    5 ——————— Ground ———————————————— 7
    6 ——————— Data Set Ready ——————————— 20
    8   Clear To Send
    7 ——————— Ready To Send —————————— 8
```

FIGURE 8-4   Wiring of a Typical Printer 9- to 25-pin RS232 Cable

The cable seems to be a simple thing, and the connector pin numbering is easy to understand. To get the right cable, just match the connectors with the same number of pins, male to female. So why doesn't every computer work properly with every peripheral? There are a number of variations, often caused by manufacturers using nonstandard pin assignments. In order to understand what is going on, let's look at some of the signals and see what they do.

RS-232C Signals

The signals that appear on each of the pins of the RS232 interface are shown in Table 8-1. Only the signals that conform to the industry standards and are common to most typical equipment are shown. If your computer or peripheral equipment has specialized applications, you may have to change your cable wiring accordingly. In the table, the Pin column shows both 25- and 9-pin connector pin numbering (the 25-pin numbering is shown first, followed by a / and the 9-pin numbering).

Normally, of the 25 pins of the DB-25 connector, only ten pins are used. These provide two grounds (FG/PG and SG), a transmit (TXD) and receive (RXD) line, two lines on each end that signal that the equipment has power and is ready to transmit and

TABLE 8-1   RS232 Pins and Signal Names

Pin 25/9	EIA Pin	Name	Description
1	AA	FG/PG	Frame or Protective Ground
2/3	BA	TXD	Transmit Data
3/2	BB	RXD	Receive Data
4/7	CA	RTS	Ready to Send
5/8	CB	CTS	Clear To Send
6/6	CC	DSR	Data Set Ready
7/5	AB	SG	Signal Ground
8/1	CF	DCD	Data Carrier Detect
9	—		Positive DC Test Voltage
10	—		Negative DC Test Voltage
11			
12	(S)CF	SDCD	Secondary Data Carrier Detect
13	(S)CB	SCTS	Secondary Clear To Send
14	(S)BA	STD	Secondary Transmit Data
15	DB	TC	Transmitter Clock
16	(S)BB	SRD	Secondary Receive Data
17	DD	RC	Receiver Clock
18			
19	(S)CA	SRTS	Secondary Ready To Send
20/4	CD	DTR	Data Terminal Ready
21	CG	SQ	Signal Quality
22/9	CE	RI	Ring Indicator
23	CH/CI		Data Rate Selector
24	DA	TC	External Transmitter Clock
25			

receive data (RTS, CTS, DSR, and DCD), and two to indicate the status of an incoming modem call (DTR and RI). On the 9-pin DE-9 connector, there is only one ground (SG) leaving eight pins to provide signal connections.

With the caveat that a few manufacturers of computers and modems may use the RS-232 standard signal lines differently, these lines are defined in the following paragraphs.

PG—Protective Ground

The PG Signal is the chassis ground for the computer, the printer, or the modem. This line ties the grounds together to reduce the possibility of shock. The protective ground signal does not appear on a DE-9 9-pin connector.

TXD—Transmit Data

The TXD signal is the actual data signal being transmitted from one piece of equipment to the other. On the other end, this signal is the RXD (Receive Data) signal connected to the RXD pin of that connector.

RXD—Receive Data

The RXD signal is the data signal that is being received from the other piece of equipment. On the other end, this signal is the TXD (Transmit Data) signal.

Note: The TXD and RXD signals, along with the Signal Ground, are the only lines required for data communications. All the other lines are used for control or handshaking.

RTS—Ready To Send

The RTS signal is output by the computer to a modem or printer to indicate that the computer is ready to send data.

CTS—Clear To Send

The CTS signal is output by the modem or printer to the computer to indicate that the modem may send data to the computer.

DSR—Data Set Ready

The DSR signal is sent from the modem to the computer or terminal, indicating that the modem is ready to be used. Typically this signal indicates that the modem has power applied and has successfully performed its initialization (internal setup) routines.

SG—Signal Ground

The SG signal is the ground reference for the various signals transmitted on the RS232 cable. Although under normal conditions in a 25-pin connector, SG may be the same as the PG signal, this is not always the case. These two signals, SG and PG, should never be tied together in the cable; they may be tied only in the equipment, and only by design of the engineer. The protective ground signal (pin 1 in a 25-pin connector) does not appear in a 9-pin connector.

DCD—Data Carrier Detect

The DCD signal, sent by a modem to a terminal or computer, indicates that the modem has received a carrier signal from a modem on the far end of the telephone line.

DTR—Data Terminal Ready

The DTR signal is sent from the computer or terminal to the modem, indicating that the computer is ready to be used. Usually this signal indicates that the computer has power applied.

RI—Ring Indicator

The RI signal, sent by a modem to a terminal or computer, indicates that there is a phone call coming in. This signal is the electrical equivalent of the telephone ringing. When the computer receives this signal, it usually sends an interrupt to activate the program or routines that answer incoming calls.

Typical Communications

The following four steps are a simplification of the procedure the computer and a peripheral device use to get information transferred from one piece of equipment to the other. The pieces of equipment in this example are a computer and a printer, both using 25-pin connectors.

1. The computer looks at DTR, pin 20, to determine whether the printer is turned on. Normally, the printer turns DTR ON when power is applied to the printer.

2. At the same time, the printer looks at DSR, pin 6, to determine if the computer is turned on. Normally, the computer turns DSR ON when power is applied to the computer.
   NOTE: At this point, if either of the above checks shows the other end is turned off, further attempts at communication are halted. The means of signaling the user that this condition exists varies, and in some equipment this check is ignored or not even made.

3. The computer then begins sending data to the printer. This is sent over the TXD line, pin 2.

4. At some point, the printer will have received more data than it can print since the computer is sending the data at several hundred characters per second. At this time, the printer signals the computer to stop sending data. This is done with RTS, pin 4. So long as the printer sets pin 4 active, the computer waits. When RTS goes off, the computer begins to send more data.

It is relatively simple, except for a few complications. For example:

- When connecting a modem to a computer, you might want the modem to signal the computer when a call is being received. This function is handled with the RI line, pin 22. When it goes ON, the computer knows that there is a call coming in, and it can then set up its software to answer the call and converse with the caller. Normally, this pin is not used for any other application.

• When a modem is used to communicate with another computer with a modem, how do we tell the computer (or terminal) that the modems have connected with each other? This function is handled with the DCD line, pin 8. When this pin is ON, the computer knows that the two modems are talking. Normally, this pin is not used for any other application.

• Also, when using a modem, the modem must tell the computer that it is ready to send data. The computer will then send the characters to the modem one at a time. The CTS line usually turns ON and OFF on a character-by-character basis.

Now that we have covered some of the communications procedures or protocols that you might encounter, let's look at how the connectors are configured.

Connector Configurations

The pin numbers in Table 8-1 are for a connector configuration often referred to as a DTE (Data Terminal Equipment) pinout. The connector to which this mates has a DCE (Data Communications Equipment) pinout. This means that some of the pins on the connector are functionally different. Pins on one type of equipment are sending the signal where pins on the other type of equipment are trying to receive it. One reason you may have trouble hooking equipment together is that the standard differs between types of equipment.

To try to simplify this, suppose that you want to connect a terminal to a modem. When one of the units is transmitting on pin 2, the other unit must be receiving on pin 2. The same for pin 3. The modem must have a DCE configuration to allow this to happen. An example of this is shown in Figure 8-5.

There may be more signals required than just the two shown in Figure 8-5, but we'll ignore these for now. Since a terminal

```
Computer                                        Modem
Connector                                       Connector
   3 ———————— Transmit Data ———————— 2
   2 ———————— Receive Data ————————— 3
   5 ———————— Signal Ground ———————— 7
```

FIGURE 8-5   TXD/RXD Signal Wiring

```
9-pin
Computer                                        Printer
Connector                                       Connector
   1 ———————— Carrier Detect ———————— 4
   2 ———————— Receive Data ————————— 2
   3 ———————— Transmit Data ————————— 3
   4 ——————— Data Terminal Ready ——————— 5
                                              6
   5 ———————————— Ground ——————————— 7
   6 —————————— Data Set Ready ———————— 20
   8 —— Clear To Send
   7 ————————— Ready To Send ————————— 8
```

FIGURE 8-6   Null Modem Cable Wiring

normally has a DTE configuration, it is transmitting on pin 2 and receiving on pin 3. The modem should be wired accordingly, receiving on pin 2 and transmitting on pin 3. The modem therefore has a DCE configuration.

The other signal lines operate on the same principle. When one piece of equipment is sending a signal, the other piece should be configured to receive it.

Now, what happens if both of the pieces of equipment you are using have a DTE configuration? What if they are both a DCE configuration? How do you make them "talk"?

One of the ways this is accomplished is with a special cable called a null modem. This is a cable that, normally, crosses the wiring between pins 2 & 3, 4 & 5, and 6 & 20. The effect of a null modem cable is to allow both of the devices interconnected to be a DTE (or DCE) configuration, and yet they can both transmit (or receive) on the same pin. The wiring of this cable is shown in Figure 8-6.

When you want to connect two computers together, such as a laptop and a desktop computer, the fastest way to transfer data is to connect them with a direct-connect cable as shown schematically in Figure 8-7 (25-pin) and Figure 8-8 (9-pin). Using this method, you can usually transfer files at high speed. You can use the operating system **mode** command or other utility program to set the port baud rate to 19,200 (or often even higher). There are many communications programs designed for file transfer, both commercial programs and some public-domain programs available from bulletin boards. Any communication utility program designed to work with a modem should work with direct connection, and usually at a much higher speed.

Just as some equipment is normally configured for DTE connections, some equipment is normally configured for DCE connections. Typical connector configurations are:

Computer Connector		Computer Connector
1	Cable Ground	1
2	Transmit Data	3
3	Receive Data	2
7	Ground	7
5 & 6	Carrier Detect	20
20	Data Terminal Ready	5 & 6

FIGURE 8-7 Wiring of a Typical Computer-to-Computer 25-pin RS232 Cable

Computer Connector		Computer Connector
1	Cable Ground	1
3	Transmit Data	2
2	Receive Data	3
7	Ground	7
6 & 8	Carrier Detect	4
4	Data Terminal Ready	6 & 8

FIGURE 8-8 Wiring of a Typical Computer-to-Computer 9-pin RS232 Cable

Equipment	Configuration
Computer	
printer port	DTE or DCE
modem port	DTE
terminal port	DTE or DCE
Modem	DCE
Printer	DTE
Terminal	DTE

The following list shows some of the names used when talking about the signal levels on the RS232 interface. Which is the "right" one or the "wrong" one seems to be up to the individual manufacturer. The best that can be done here is to present as many of the common terms as possible with their equivalents in the same column, then let you determine which ones you will use. Note that the EIA specification uses the terms "On" and "Off." By using these terms, you can be assured of at least adhering to the EIA standard which defines the RS232 interface.

Term	Opposite State
Zero	One
$> +3$ Volts	< -3 Volts
$+12$ Volts	-12 Volts
Positive	Negative
Reset	Set
Space	Mark
Off	On
On	Off
Lo	Hi
Open	Closed
Break	
Perforation	No Perforation
Active	Inactive

Start	Stop
False	True
Binary 0	Binary 1

Some of the terms above seem to be contradictory (for example, ON and OFF), indicating how much the standard has been ignored. All of the above terms come from popular manufacturers of computers, modems, printers, and terminals.

Serial Data Format

Data format is not part of the RS232 specification because the serial interface specification only addresses the connector that delivers the data and not the format of the data. But since it is such an integral part of serial data communications, you may need the information here together with the other serial port information when setting up a serial communications link.

The serial data stream consists of a start bit, the actual data bits (usually 5, 6, 7 or 8 bits), an optional parity bit, and a stop bit (usually 1 bit, but can be 1.5 or 2 bits). This is shown in Figure 8-9.

In the same way that the hardware connections must be made to match, both the computer and the peripheral have to be

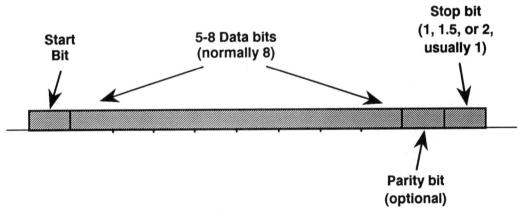

FIGURE 8-9   Serial Data Stream Format

set to the same data format options for everything to work properly. For example, a modem typically is set for 8 data bits, no parity bit, and 1 stop bit. This is often abbreviated 8,N,1. Look in your peripheral manual to determine what the peripheral uses. Once you have determined the data format the peripheral uses, you can use a software program to set the computer port to the proper format to match it. Usually on an EISA machine, this is set with the installation program. However, if the EISA installation program does not provide a means of setting the serial port (or ports), you can use the PC/MS-DOS operating system **mode** command to set the port. Refer to your PC/MS-DOS operating system manual and the computer documentation for the specifics of your particular system.

A few notes:

- A modem should almost always be set for 8 data bits. Setting the modem for 7 or less will result in loss of data, especially when using the modem to download software, since all software is 8 bits wide and using 7-bit mode will garble the files.

- A printer will not always require 8 bits, since most of the data sent to it is 7-bit ASCII information. However, some printers require the eighth bit for control information, and others are confused by the eighth bit. Be sure to consult the printer manual.

- You should usually set the printer to as high a speed as possible, since many printers actually receive more than one character for each character they print. The additional characters are control characters for some of the printer's functions such as bold printing, font changes, and so forth.

- Sometimes printers garble the printing because they are receiving the characters faster than they can process them. Although most printers have good "handshaking" between the printer and the computer to help eliminate this problem, some lack this sophistication. If you are having a problem, first shift the printer (and the computer's serial port) to a low speed such as 300 baud and see if the problem persists. Handshaking problems usually show up at speeds above 2400 baud.

Serial I/O Ports and Interrupts

The serial output port (or ports) on most EISA computers can be set up as Port 1, 2, 3 or 4. These ports are mapped to different I/O addresses and have different interrupt levels as shown below:

Port	I/O Address	Interrupt Level
1	3F8h–3FFh	4
2	2F8h–2FFh	3
3	3E8h–3EFh	10
4	2E8h–2EFh	11

A typical EISA computer will have at least one serial port, and two is not uncommon. Additional serial ports are easily added through cards that plug into the EISA backplane. These cards usually add either one parallel port and one serial port, or two serial ports. The addition of the card is handled by the EISA software and once the software has added the card to its inventory, your computer can easily have up to four serial ports for modems, printers, data communications links with other computers, or terminals for multi-user systems.

Serial Port Registers

The serial port of most EISA computers has 11 registers. Table 8-2 lists the registers and their addresses.

Transmit Buffer Register

The Transmit Buffer register holds the data to be sent out on the TXD pin on the serial connector. Data bit 0, the least-significant

TABLE 8-2   Serial Port Subsystem Registers

Register	Port 1	Port 2	Port 3	Port 4
Transmit Buffer	3F8h	2F8h	3E8h	2E8h
Receive Buffer	3F8h	2F8h	3E8h	2E8h
Divisor Latch LSB	3F8h	2F8h	3E8h	2E8h
Divisor Latch MSB	3F9h	2F9h	3E9h	2E9h
Interrupt Enable	3F9h	2F9h	3E9h	2E9h
Interrupt ID	3FAh	2FAh	3EAh	2EAh
Line Control	3FBh	2FBh	3EBh	2EBh
Modem Control	3FCh	2FCh	3ECh	2ECh
Line Status	3FDh	2FDh	3EDh	2EDh
Modem Status	3FEh	2FEh	3EEh	2EEh
Reserved	3FFh	2FFh	3EFh	2EFh

bit (LSB), is sent first and data bit 7, the most-significant bit (MSB), is sent last.

Receive Buffer Register

The Receive Buffer register contains the characters received on the RXD pin on the serial connector. Data bit 0 (LSB) is received first and data bit 7 (MSB) is received last.

Divisor Latch Registers

The Divisor Latch registers control the baud rate of the transmitted and received data. Table 8-3 shows the values loaded into the Divisor Latch registers to set the baud rate.

Bit 7 of the Line Control register determines whether the Divisor Latch MSB or the Interrupt Enable register is accessed.

TABLE 8-3   Divisor Latch Values

Baud	MSB Bits								Bits LSB							
Rate	7	6	5	4	3	2	1	0	7	6	5	4	3	2	1	0
75	0	0	0	0	0	1	1	0	0	0	0	0	0	0	0	0
110	0	0	0	0	0	1	0	0	0	0	0	1	0	1	1	1
300	0	0	0	0	0	0	0	1	1	0	0	0	0	0	0	0
600	0	0	0	0	0	0	0	0	1	1	0	0	0	0	0	0
1200	0	0	0	0	0	0	0	0	0	1	1	0	0	0	0	0
2400	0	0	0	0	0	0	0	0	0	0	1	1	0	0	0	0
4800	0	0	0	0	0	0	0	0	0	0	0	1	1	0	0	0
9600	0	0	0	0	0	0	0	0	0	0	0	0	1	1	0	0
19200	0	0	0	0	0	0	0	0	0	0	0	0	0	1	1	0

Interrupt Enable Register

The Interrupt Enable register enables and disables the four types of interrupts.

Bit	Data	Interrupt
0	1	Enables the Received Data Available interrupt.
	0	Disables the interrupt.
1	1	Enables the Transmitter Holding Register Empty interrupt.
	0	Disables the interrupt.
2	1	Enables the Receiver Line Status interrupt.
	0	Disables the interrupt.
3	1	Enables the Modem Status interrupt.
	0	Disables interrupt.
4-7		Should always be 0.

Interrupt Identification Register

The Interrupt Identification register identifies the highest priority pending interrupt signal. When this register is addressed, it inhibits the highest priority interrupt. No other interrupts are acknowledged until this inhibited interrupt is cleared.

Bit	Data	Definition
0	0	An interrupt is pending.
1-2		Identify the pending interrupt with the highest priority:

Bit		Interrupt
1	2	
1	1	Receiver line status
1	0	Received data available
0	1	Transmit buffer empty
0	0	Modem status

Bit	Data	Definition
3-7		Should always be 0.

Line Control Register

The Line Control register controls the format of the data communications.

Bit	Data	Definition
0-1		Specify the number of bits in each transmitted or received character:

Bit		Character Length in Bits
0	1	
1	1	8
1	0	7
0	1	6
0	0	5

2	0	One stop bit is generated or deleted in the data sent or received.
	1	For 5-bit words 1.5 stop bits are generated or deleted. For a 6, 7, or 8-bit word, 2 stop bits are generated or deleted.
3	0	Disables the parity bit.
	1	A parity bit is generated (transmit data) or checked (receive data).
4	0	When bit 3 is 0, the parity bits sent or checked are odd.
	1	When bit 3 is 1, the parity bits sent or checked are even.
5	1	When bit 3 is 1, the parity bit is 0 for even parity and 1 for odd parity.
	0	The stuck parity is disabled.
6	1	Sets the transmit data line to the space state (0) and remains at that state regardless of the state of the output buffer register.
	0	Set-breaking is disabled.
7	1	Address selection bit. It is set to gain access to the divisor latches of the baud-rate generator during a read/write operation.
	0	Reset to gain access to the Receiver Buffer register, the Transmit Buffer register, or the Interrupt Enable register.

Modem Control Register

The Modem Control register controls the modem signals and allows the serial port to be set to a diagnostic mode. The receiver and transmitter interrupts and the modem control interrupts are fully operational, allowing the interrupts to be tested.

Bit	Data	Definition
0	1	DTR (Data Terminal Ready) signal is active.
	0	DTR signal is inactive.
1	1	RTS (Request To Send) signal is active.
	0	RTS signal is inactive.
2		Controls the OUT1˜ signal from the controller chip. It can be 0 or 1.
3	1	Controls OUT2˜ signal from the controller chip.
	0	Forces the OUT2˜ output inactive.
4	1	Enables the modem loopback (diagnostic test) as follows:

> The transmitter serial input is disabled.
>
> Transmitter serial output is set to the active state.
>
> The output from the transmitter shift register is looped back to the receiver shift register.
>
> The four modem control inputs to the modem status register are disabled.
>
> The four modem control outputs from the modem control register are internally connected to the four modem control inputs.

Bit	Data	Definition
5-7		Should always be 0.

Line Status Register

The Line Status register provides information on the data transfer. Bits 1 through 4 are error conditions that generate a receiver line status interrupt.

Bit	Data	Definition
0	1	A complete incoming character has been received and is in the Receiver Buffer register.
	0	Reset by reading the data in the Receiver Buffer register or writing a 0 in it.
1	1	Data in the Receive Buffer register was not read by the processor before the next character was transferred into the register.
	0	Reset when the CPU reads the Line Status register.
2	1	Parity error detected.
	0	Reset when the CPU reads the Line Status register.
3	1	Framing error has occurred.
	0	Reset when the CPU reads the Line Status register.
4	1	Received data line was at a space state (0) for longer than the transmission time of a complete data character.
	0	Reset when the CPU reads the Line Status register.
5	1	Character is transferred from the Transmit Buffer register to the Transmit Shift register.
	0	Reset when the next character is written into the Transmit Buffer register.
6	1	Transmit Buffer register and Transmit Shift register are empty.
	0	Reset when either register contains a character.
7		Should always be 0.

Modem Status Register

The Modem Status register provides information on the control lines from the modem or device.

Bit	Data	Definition
0	1	CTS (Clear To Send) signal input changed state.
	0	Reset when the Modem Status register is read.
1	1	DSR (Data Set Ready) input changed state.
	0	Reset when the Modem Status register is read.
2	1	RI (Ring Indicator) input changed from a low to a high state.
	0	Reset when the Modem Status register is read.
3	1	DCD (Data Carrier Detect) input changed state.
	0	Reset when the Modem Status register is read.
4	1	CTS (Clear To Send) input is active.
	0	CTS input is inactive.
5	1	DSR (Data Set Ready) input is active.
	0	DSR input is inactive.
6	1	RI (Ring Indicator) input is active.
	0	RI input is inactive.
7	1	CF input is active.
	0	CF input is inactive.

Serial Port BIOS Routines

The BIOS of most EISA computers provides six functions which are used to output and receive data through the serial port. These functions can be divided into two categories: those that provide or control protocol or status, and those that transmit and receive data. These functions are:

Function	Equate	Definition
00	INIT	Initialize Serial Port
01	XMIT	Send Out One Character
02	RECV	Receive One Character
03	STATUS	Get Serial Port Status
04	EXTENDED_INIT	Extended Serial Port Initialization

INIT

The INIT function sets the baud rate, number of stop bits, parity and character length of the specified serial port. It returns with the contents of the Line Status register and the Modem Status register of the specified port.

```
On Entry: AH = F14_INIT (00h)
          AL = Port attribute

          Bit   Data  Definition

          7-5   111    9600 baud rate
                110    4800 baud rate
                101    2400 baud rate
                100    1200 baud rate
                011    600 baud rate
                010    300 baud rate
                001    150 baud rate
                000    110 baud rate
          4-3   x0     no parity
                11     even parity
                01     odd parity
          2     0      1 stop bit
                1      2 stop bits
          1-0   00     5 bits
                01     6 bits
                10     7 bit character
                11     8 bit character
```

```
        DX = Port number

On Exit: AH = Line Status
         AL = Modem Status


Registers Altered: AX
```

The following defines the Line Status byte as returned in the AH register:

Bit	Data	Definition
7	1	Timeout Error
6	1	Transmit Shift Register Empty
5	1	Transmit Hold Register Empty
4	1	Break Received
3	1	Character Framing Error
2	1	Parity Error
1	1	Overrun Error
0	1	Data Set Ready

The following defines the Modem Status byte as returned in the AL register:

Bit	Data	Definition
7	1	Receive Line Signal Detected
6	1	Ring Indicator Line State
5	1	Data Set Ready Line State
4	1	Clear to Send Line State
3	1	Change in Receive Line Detected
2	1	Trailing Edge of Ring Detected
1	1	Change in Data Set Ready
0	1	Change in Clear to Send State

A printer connected to the serial port would typically operate at 9600 baud with no parity, use two stop bits, and require 8-bit characters (to allow the passage of control characters). The following shows the programming of the serial port for these parameters:

Example:

```
MOV AH, INIT      ; AH = 00h
MOV AL, 11100111B ; 9600 baud, No parity, 2 stop bits, 8 bit
MOV DX, 1         ; Send it to port 1
INT 14h           ; Call the serial driver using INT 14h
```

XMIT

The XMIT function transmits a byte of data through the serial port defined by the DX register.

```
On Entry: AH = XMIT (01h)
          AL = Data byte to be sent
          DX = Port number

On Exit: AH = Line status
         AL = Modem status


Registers Altered: AX
```

RECV

The RECV function reads a byte of data from the serial port defined by the DX register.

```
On Entry: AH = RECV (02h)
          DX = Port number

On Exit: AH = Line status
         AL = If no error: Data byte received


If error: Null character, zero


Registers Altered: AX
```

STATUS

The STATUS function provides the status of the serial port defined by the DX register.

```
On Entry: AH = STATUS (03h)
          DX = Port number

On Exit: AH = Line status
         AL = Modem status


Registers Altered: AX
```

EXTENDED_INIT

The EXTENDED_INIT function sets the break, parity, stop bits, word length, and baud rate for the defined serial port. This function provides more choices than those in F14_INIT, but requires more extensive data in the various registers.

```
On Entry: AH = EXTENDED_INIT
          AL = Break
               00h = No Break
               01h = Break
          BH = Parity
               00h = None
               01h = Odd
               02h = Even
               03h = Stick parity odd
               04h = Stick parity even
          BL = Stop bit
               00h = One
               01h = Two if 6-, 7-, or 8-bit word length
                     One and one half if 5-bit word length
          CH = Word Length
               00h = 5 bits
               01h = 6 bits
               02h = 7 bits
               03h = 8 bits
          CL = Baud rate
               00h = 110 baud
               01h = 150 baud
```

```
                        02h = 300 baud
                        03h = 600 baud
                        04h = 1200 baud
                        05h = 2400 baud
                        06h = 4800 baud
                        07h = 9600 baud
                        08h = 19200 baud
```

Programming Examples

Initialize Serial Port

```
;
;   The following program uses the BIOS to initialize the serial port
;   for modem communication.  Though this is just a code fragment, it
;   can be assembled, linked, and run from MS-DOS.
;

_TEXT       SEGMENT BYTE PUBLIC 'CODE'
_TEXT       ENDS

_DATA       SEGMENT WORD PUBLIC 'DATA'
_DATA       ENDS

_DATA       SEGMENT
_DATA       ENDS


_TEXT       SEGMENT
            ASSUME      CS:_TEXT


            ;
            ; Initialize the serial port - assume COM1 will be used.
            ;
            mov         dx,00h          ;Set serial port number: 0 = COM1
            mov         ah,00h          ;Set serial initialization function
            mov         al,10100011b    ;Set 2400 baud, no parity,
                                        ; 8 data bits, 1 stop bit
            int         14H             ;Invoke BIOS to initialize serial port

            ;
```

```
                       ; Exit back to DOS.
                       ;
                       mov        ax,4C00h
                       int        21h


_TEXT          ENDS
               END
```

Read Serial Port Status

```
;
;  The following code fragment uses the BIOS to read the serial
;  port status.  Though this is just a code fragment, it can be
;  assembled, linked, and run from MS-DOS.
;
_TEXT          SEGMENT BYTE PUBLIC 'CODE'
_TEXT          ENDS


_DATA          SEGMENT WORD PUBLIC 'DATA'
_DATA          ENDS



_DATA          SEGMENT
_DATA          ENDS



_TEXT          SEGMENT
               ASSUME     CS:_TEXT


                       ;
                       ; Initialize the serial port - assume COM1 will be used
                       ;
                       mov        dx,00h              ;Set serial port number: 0 = COM1
                       mov        ah,00h              ;Set serial initialization function
                       mov        al,10100011b        ;Set 2400 baud, no parity,
                                                      ; 8 data bits, 1 stop bit
                       int        14H                 ;Invoke BIOS to initialize serial port

                       ;          .
                       ;          .
                       ;          .
```

```
                ;
                ; Initialize the serial port - assume COM1 will be used
                ;
                mov        dx,00h          ;Set serial port number: 0 = COM1
                mov        ah,03h          ;Set serial status function
                int        14H             ;Invoke BIOS to get status - modem
                                           ; status back in AL, line status in AH

                ;            .
                ;            .
                ;            .


                ;
                ; Exit back to DOS.
                ;
                mov        ax,4C00h
                int        21h

_TEXT           ENDS
                END
```

Send/Receive Character From Serial Port

```
;
;  The following code fragment uses the BIOS to send a character
;  to the serial port and receive a character from the serial port.
;  It is merely a code fragment, and it should not be run.
;

_TEXT           SEGMENT BYTE PUBLIC 'CODE'
_TEXT           ENDS

_DATA           SEGMENT WORD PUBLIC 'DATA'
_DATA           ENDS



_DATA           SEGMENT
_DATA           ENDS



_TEXT           SEGMENT
                ASSUME     CS:_TEXT
```

```
        ;
        ; Initialize the serial port - assume COM1 will be used
        ;
        mov         dx,00h              ;Set serial port number: 0 = COM1
        mov         ah,00h              ;Set serial initialization function
        mov         al,10100011b        ;Set 2400 baud, no parity,
                                        ; 8 data bits, 1 stop bit
        int         14H                 ;Invoke BIOS to initialize serial port

        ;           .
        ;           .
        ;           .


        ;
        ; Output an "A" to the serial port.
        ;
        mov         dx,00h              ;Set serial port number: 0 = COM1
        mov         ah,01h              ;Set serial output character function
        mov         al,"A"             ;Set character to output
        int         14H                 ;Invoke BIOS to output character

        ;           .
        ;           .
        ;           .


        ;
        ; Get a character from the serial port.
        ;
        mov         dx,00h              ;Set serial port number: 0 = COM1
        mov         ah,02h              ;Set serial input character function
        int         14H                 ;Invoke BIOS to input character

        ;           .
        ;           .
        ;           .


        ;
        ; Exit back to DOS.
        ;
        mov         ax,4C00h
        int         21h

_TEXT   ENDS
        END
```

Summary

Most of the EISA machines are supplied with two serial ports for the connection of printers, modems, or other serial devices. The EISA computers maintain the addresses and interrupts as defined in the previous ISA standard, so that using existing software and programming expertise with the peripheral interfaces of the EISA computers is possible.

CHAPTER
9

The Parallel Printer Connector

This chapter covers the parallel printer interface port found on a typical EISA computer system. The emphasis is on using the parallel port interface for connecting printers to the computer system, though the parallel port is also sometimes used for other peripherals such as an 8-bit controller, or for high-speed data transfer.

The parallel interface uses signal levels at standard TTL logic levels. This means that the cable lengths are somewhat less than those of serial interfaces—in fact, parallel cables are usually about 25 feet long or less because of wire resistance and the low voltage levels found in the parallel interface. Typical hardware line drivers will have the following characteristics:

Sink Current   24 mA maximum

Source Current   15 mA maximum

Logic High Output Voltage   2.4 Vdc minimum

Logic Low Output Voltage   0.5 Vdc maximum

Note that these levels are typical. Different computer manufacturers may use drivers that do not provide these exact values, especially on pins 1, 14, 16, and 17. If you are using an interface that may be nonstandard, such as might be found in a computer not from a major manufacturer, you should consult the technical reference manual of the computer or interface to make sure that your levels are compatible.

The Parallel Port Connector

Normally, the parallel port connector on the back of the computer is a female, 25-pin, D-type connector. Figure 9-1 shows the pin numbers as they appear on the equipment connector. Note that the pin numbering is a mirror image as you look at the cable end, though the numbers on the cable connector are the same.

In a normal configuration, a female connector is mounted on the equipment and the male connector is mounted on the cable. The printer end of the cable has a Centronics-type connector, a 36-pin connector, as shown in Figure 9-2. The wiring of a typical cable is shown in Figure 9-3.

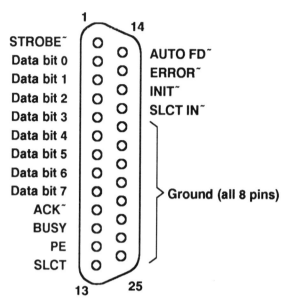

FIGURE 9-1   Parallel Printer Connector Pin Numbering

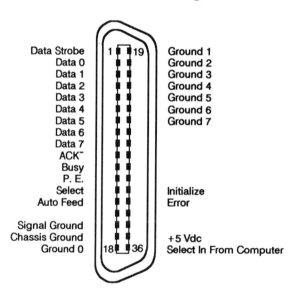

FIGURE 9-2   Typical Centronics Connector Pin Numbering

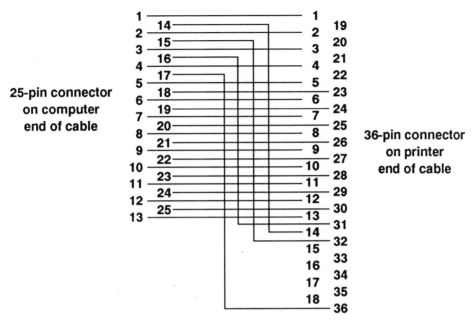

25-pin connector on computer end of cable

36-pin connector on printer end of cable

FIGURE 9-3   Typical Parallel Printer Cable Wiring

Parallel Printer Signals

The signals that appear on each of the pins of the Parallel interface are defined in Table 9-1. Only the signals that conform to the industry standards and are common to most typical equipment are shown. If your computer has a nonstandard connector arrangement, you will have to make cable changes or purchase appropriate cables from the computer manufacturer.

Signal Timing

The signals on the connector must conform to certain timing restrictions. There are three control signals, BUSY, ACK˜, and STROBE˜, that are coordinated with the 8 data lines. These signals, and the nominal timing requirements, are shown in Figure 9-4.

Parallel Port Addresses/Registers

The parallel output port can be addressed as parallel port 1, 2, or 3. Port selection is usually accomplished by the installation pro-

TABLE 9-1 Parallel Port Pin Assignments

Pin	I/O	Signal	Definition
1	O	STROBE~	Data strobe
2	O	D0	Data bit 0
3	O	D1	Data bit 1
4	O	D2	Data bit 2
5	O	D3	Data bit 3
6	O	D4	Data bit 4
7	O	D5	Data bit 5
8	O	D6	Data bit 6
9	O	D7	Data bit 7
10	I	ACK~	Printer acknowledges receipt of the character and is ready for the next character.
11	I	BUSY	Printer is busy and is not ready to accept more data.
12	I	PE	Printer error; usually means the printer is out of paper.
13	I	SLCT	Printer select.
14	O	AUTO FD~	Tells printer to perform a linefeed after a line is printed.
15	I	ERROR~	Printer has encountered an error.
16	O	INIT~	Initializes the printer.
17	O	SLCT IN~	Enables the printer for printing.
18	GND	Ground	
19	GND	Ground	
20	GND	Ground	
21	GND	Ground	
22	GND	Ground	
23	GND	Ground	
24	GND	Ground	
25	GND	Ground	

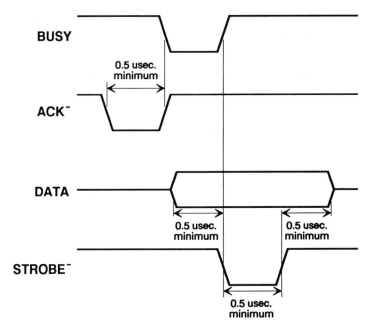

FIGURE 9-4   Typical Parallel Connector Timing

gram which sets up the EISA computer. Information on how to use this setup software is presented in Chapter 6, *EISA Software*. Each of the ports is mapped to a different I/O address as follows:

	Port		
Register	**1**	**2**	**3**
Data Address	03BCh	0378h	0278h
Status Address	03BDh	0379h	0279h
Control Address	03BEh	037Ah	027Ah

Characters can be output through the parallel port in two ways. The first way uses the BIOS routines to output the data; this is the preferable method, and will result in optimum compatibility between different computer manufacturers. This is shown later in this chapter. The second way is to output the data directly to the port at the addresses shown above; this is usually a faster way, since it bypasses the BIOS routines, but it risks incompatibility. The parallel output registers may be located at a different, non-standard address. The information normally contained in these registers is described in the following paragraphs.

Data Register

The Data register contains the data to be sent to the printer. Writing a character to this register causes it to be sent to the equipment or device connected to the parallel port.

Printer Control Register

The Printer Control register controls the printer signals by loading the CPU register with the appropriate data from that shown in the following bit definition table, and then outputting the byte to the Printer Control register.

Bit	Data	Definition
0	1	Generates an active low STROBE signal for at least 500nS. The STROBE signal is used to clock the data from the parallel port into the printer. Note that the data must be on the DATA pins at least $0.5\mu S$ before and after the STROBE signal.
	0	STROBE inactive.
1	1	Generates the low AUTO FD~ signal; printer automatically does a line feed after each line is printed.
	0	AUTO FD~ signal inactive.
2	0	Generates the low INIT~ signal for at least $50\mu S$; printer initializes (prepares itself for operation.)
	1	INIT~ signal inactive.
3	1	Generates the low SLCT IN~ signal; printer is selected and ready for use.
	0	SLCT IN signal inactive; printer deselected or inactive.

4	1	Enables the printer parallel port interrupt when the ACK~ input signals that the printer is ready.
	0	ACK~ input signal inactive.
5	1	Controls the direction of the printer port. In some computers, this bit can be used to set up the parallel port as a bidirectional port, allowing the parallel port to read data as well as output it to a device such as a printer.
6,7		Not used. Usually tagged as reserved.

Printer Status Register

The Printer Status register provides information on the control lines coming from the printer.

Bit	Data	Definition
0-1		Not used. Usually tagged as reserved.
2	0	Printer has acknowledged receipt of the data with the ACK signal.
	1	ACK signal inactive.
3	0	ERROR~ input active and an error condition exists.
	1	ERROR~ input inactive.
4	1	SLCT input active; printer has been selected.
	0	SLCT input inactive.
5	1	PE input active; typically, the printer is out of paper.
	0	PE input inactive.
6	0	ACK~ input active; printer ready to accept data.
	1	ACK~ input inactive.
7	0	BUSY input active; printer cannot receive data.
	1	BUSY input inactive.

Parallel Port BIOS Routines

The BIOS of most EISA computers provides three functions that are used to output characters on the parallel port. These functions are:

Function	Equate	Definition
00H	PUT_CHAR	Send a character to the printer
01H	INIT	Initialize the printer port
02H	STATUS	Get the printer port status

PUT_CHAR

The PUT_CHAR function sends a character to the parallel port. It returns with the port status in the AH register.

```
On Entry: AH = PUT_CHAR (00h)
          AL = Data byte to be sent to printer
          DX = Port number

On Exit: AH = Printer port status

Registers Altered: AH
```

The following shows the printer port status byte as returned in the AH register.

Bit	Data	Definition
7	0	Printer Busy
	1	Printer Not Busy
6	0	Not Ready for Data
	1	Data Acknowledged
5	1	Out of Paper
4	0	Printer Offline
	1	Printer On Line

3	1	I/O Error
2,1		Not Used
0	1	Printer Error or Timed out

INIT

The INIT function initializes the parallel printer port. The function returns with the printer port status in the AH register in the same manner as the previous PUT_CHAR function.

```
On Entry: AH = INIT (01h)
          DX = Port number

On Exit: AH = Printer port status

Registers Altered: AH
```

STATUS

The STATUS function provides the status of the parallel printer port.

```
On Entry: AH = STATUS (02h)
          DX = Port number

On Exit: AH = Printer port status

Registers Altered: AH
```

Programming Examples

Send Character to Printer

```
;
; The following program uses the BIOS to output a character
;  to the printer.  This program can be assembled, linked, and
;  run from MS-DOS.
;
```

```
_TEXT          SEGMENT BYTE PUBLIC 'CODE'
_TEXT          ENDS


_DATA          SEGMENT WORD PUBLIC 'DATA'
_DATA          ENDS


LPT_STATUS_MASK_ERROR      EQU 000010000b;LPT Status mask for ERROR


LF             EQU          0Ah           ;Line feed
FF             EQU          0Ch           ;Form feed
CR             EQU          0Dh           ;Carriage return



_DATA          SEGMENT


LptMsgNotReady                        DB 'The printer is not ready',CR,LF,0


_DATA          ENDS



_TEXT          SEGMENT
               ASSUME       CS:_TEXT


               mov          ax,_DATA
               mov          ds,ax
               ASSUME       ds:_DATA


LPT1
               ;
               ; Initialize the printer port - assume
               ; the printer is attached to LPT1.
               ;
               mov          dx,00h        ;Set printer port number: 0 =
               mov          ah,01h        ;Set printer initialization function
               int          17h           ;Invoke BIOS to initialize port


               ;
               ; Check the printer status.
               ;
               xor          cx,cx         ;Set printer status wait count
```

```
lpt_10:
          mov          dx,00h            ;Set printer port number: 0 = LPT1
          mov          ah,02h            ;Set printer status function
          int          17H               ;Invoke BIOS to get status

          test         ah,LPT_STATUS_MASK_ERROR

          jz           lpt_30            ;No printer errors?
          loop         lpt_10            ;Check printer status again?


          ;
          ; The printer is not ready - print an error message and quit.
          ;
lpt_15:
          mov          si,OFFSET LptMsgNotReady


lpt_20:
          lodsb                          ;Get the next error string character
          or           al,al
          jz           lpt_40            ;End of string?

          mov          ah,0Eh            ;Set BIOS write character function
          int          10h               ;Invoke BIOS to Display character

          jmp          lpt_20            ;Check for more characters


          ;
          ; Output a character to the printer.
          ;
lpt_30:
          mov          dx,00h            ;Set printer port number: 0 = LPT1
          mov          ah,00h            ;Set printer put character function
          mov          al,"A"            ;Set the character to output
          int          17H               ;Invoke BIOS to output character

          test         ah,LPT_STATUS_MASK_ERROR

          jnz          lpt_15            ;Error status back from printer?

          mov          dx,00h            ;Set printer port number: 0 = LPT1
          mov          ah,00h            ;Set printer put character function
          mov          al,FF             ;Set the form feed character
          int          17H               ;Invoke BIOS to do form feed
```

```
                ;
                ; Exit back to DOS.
                ;
lpt_40:
                mov        ax,4C00h
                int        21h

_TEXT           ENDS
                END
```

Send String to Printer

```
;
;   The following program uses the BIOS to output a string of
;   characters to the printer.  This program can be assembled,
;   linked, and run from MS-DOS.
;

_TEXT           SEGMENT BYTE PUBLIC 'CODE'
_TEXT           ENDS


_DATA           SEGMENT WORD PUBLIC 'DATA'
_DATA           ENDS


LPT_STATUS_MASK_ERROR       EQU 000010000b;LPT Status mask for ERROR

CR              EQU        0Dh             ;Carriage return
FF              EQU        0Ch             ;Form feed
LF              EQU        0Ah             ;Line feed


_DATA           SEGMENT

GoodbyeString   DB  'Good-bye',CR,LF,FF,0 ;NULL terminated Good-bye string

LptMsgNotReady  DB  'The printer is not ready',CR,LF,0  ;LPT Error string

_DATA           ENDS


_TEXT           SEGMENT
                ASSUME     CS:_TEXT
```

```
        mov         ax,_DATA
        mov         ds,ax
        ASSUME      ds:_DATA


        ;
        ; Initialize the printer port - assume
        ; the printer is attached to LPT1.
        ;
        mov         dx,00h         ;Set printer port number: 0 = LPT1
        mov         ah,01h         ;Set printer initialization function
        int         17h            ;Invoke BIOS to initialize port


        ;
        ; Check the printer status.
        ;
        xor         cx,cx          ;Set printer status wait count


lpt_10:
        mov         dx,00h         ;Set printer port number: 0 = LPT1
        mov         ah,02h         ;Set printer status function
        int         17H            ;Invoke BIOS to get status

        test        ah,LPT_STATUS_MASK_ERROR

        jz          lpt_30         ;No printer errors?
        loop        lpt_10         ;Check printer status again?


        ;
        ; The printer is not ready - print an error message and quit.
        ;
lpt_15:
        mov         si,OFFSET LptMsgNotReady


lpt_20:
        lodsb                      ;Get the next error string character
        or          al,al
        jz          lpt_40         ;End of string?

        mov         ah,0Eh         ;Set BIOS write character function
        int         10h            ;Invoke BIOS to Display character
        jmp         lpt_20         ;Check for more characters
```

```
            ;
            ; Output "Good-bye" to the printer.
            ;
lpt_30:
            mov         si,OFFSET GoodByeString

lpt_35:
            lodsb                   ;Get the next string character
            or          al,al
            jz          lpt_40      ;End of string?

            mov         dx,00h      ;Set printer port number: 0 = LPT1
            mov         ah,00h      ;Set printer put character function
            int         17H         ;Invoke BIOS to output character

            test        ah,LPT_STATUS_MASK_ERROR

            jnz         lpt_15      ;Error status back from printer?

            jmp         lpt_35      ;Check for more characters

            ;
            ; Exit back to DOS.
            ;
lpt_40:
            mov         ax,4C00h
            int         21h

_TEXT       ENDS
            END
```

Summary

The EISA computers use parallel ports that are fully compatible, both in addresses and interrupts, with the existing ISA standard. Programs and programmers using the existing standards will have no problem with the new EISA standards.

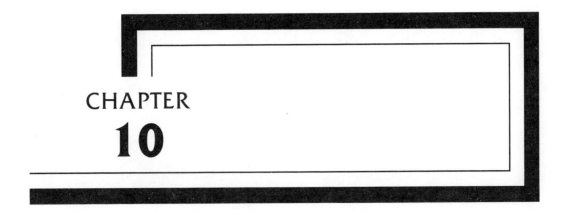

The 80486 (i486) CPU

Although the 80286 and 80386 will continue to be popular microprocessors, the i486 will undoubtedly be the processor of choice for most of the new EISA designs. The 82350 EISA chip set is an optimum match for the i486's power and features.

A word about Intel's chip names. For many years Intel has referred to their chip sets as the 8080, the 8086, the 80186, the 80286, and so forth. With the introduction of the 80486, they have changed the designations and now use just the last three digits preceded by a lower case "i." Thus, the 80386 is now often referred to as the i386, and the 80486 is now referred to as the i486. The i486 designation is used throughout the rest of this chapter.

The i486 contains all of the functionality of the 80386 (i386) and the 80387 combined in a single chip. In addition, it has a built-in cache memory that allows frequently accessed data and code to be resident in the chip, thus reducing access to the system memory.

The i486 is object-code compatible with code developed for all of the previous members of the same CPU family, including the 8086, 8088, 80186, 80188, 80286, and 80386. In addition, it features:

- Frequent instructions that execute in one clock cycle
- On-chip 8K code and data cache
- On-chip floating point (80387) coprocessor
- Paged, virtual memory management
- Built-in self test
- 25 and 33 MHz clock versions now, with faster (40 MHz) versions to come
- 106 Mbyte/second burst bus
- Performance of 37,000 Dhrystones, 6.1 million Whetstones, at 25 MHz
- Newest 1 micron CHMOS IV manufacturing technology
- All addresses, data busses, and registers are 32 bits wide
- Full support for multiprocessor operation
- 64K I/O addresses
- Addresses 4 GB of physical memory and 64 Terabytes of virtual memory

- Full support for both multitasking and multiprocessor environments
- 168-pin grid array package
- 1.18 million transistors

Intel has announced two versions of the i486, a 25 MHz version and a 33 MHz version, designated the i486-25 and the i486-33 respectively. The i486-33 is the fastest CPU available of those popular in the PC market. As more programs are written that take advantage of the internal coprocessor and memory management facilities of the i486, the speed of the i486-33 will be vastly increased over what we now consider fast and powerful computers.

Speed comparisons are difficult to make since programs can be written to take advantage of certain instructions that execute much faster in the new chip, while ignoring those that have only nominal improvements. However, even at its worst, the i486 is a major improvement over the earlier processors. In an average case, the i486-33 is approximately 4 times faster than a i386-16. The i386-16 itself is approximately 3.2 times faster than an 80286-12, which makes the i486-33 about 13 times faster than today's standard 80286 computers running at 12 MHz. A sort taking one hour on an 80286-12 computer will take four minutes on an i486 EISA computer. That, of course, ignores other possible gains made by the i486's built-in math coprocessor, the newer faster disk drives, and disk caching. If you are using one of the older IBM PC computers, the new i486 may be as much as 70 times faster.

These speed increases do not come only from an increase in clock speeds. The operation of the processor's internal circuitry is synchronized by the clock signal, which typically pulses on/off/on at the frequency indicated by the processor's clock rating. For example, a processor rated at 25 MHz would go through 25 million clock cycles per second. Some instructions take only a few clock cycles to execute, some take over 300 clock cycles to execute a single instruction. The i486 has dramatically reduced the number of clock cycles required for the execution of some instructions.

Because of the improvement in both the processor's internal architecture and in clock speeds, the i486 can perform operations that took hours on the original PCs in minutes, while operations that took minutes before now take only seconds. However, programmers are taking advantage of the power of the new processors to add many new functions and features to their software, and sometimes a state-of-the-art database running on a fast EISA machine may seem no faster than your old database program running on a PC. The newer programs are far more powerful and complex, and simply use more processor time.

Compatibility

The i486 is object-code compatible with all of the 80x86 family of processors, so that a program written for the original PC will run on the latest EISA i486 computer, for example. However, incompatibilities may occur at times. Differences in the BIOS code cause this most frequently and will represent the majority of the problems encountered. Other incompatibilities may result from the differing implementations of interrupts and interrupt controllers.

Differences also exist in the some of the opcodes and protected modes used in assembly language programming. For example, the PUSH SP instruction on the 8086 class CPUs pushes the stack pointer value after the instruction is completed, and the i486 (as well as the 80286 and 80386) push the current stack pointer. A few other instructions differ primarily in the timing of an instruction related to subsequent instructions. In most cases, assemblers such as the Microsoft assembler can take care of these differences when assembling the source code, and higher-level programming languages such as C or BASIC make the differences invisible.

The i486 has added only six new instructions, BSWAP (Byte Swap), XADD (Exchange and Add), CMPXCHG (Compare and Exchange), INVD (Invalidate), WBINVD (Write Back Invalidate), and INVLPG (Invalidate TBL Entry), as described below.

Instruction	Function
BSWAP	Reverses the order of the bits in a register to support fast translation between big endian (680x0 and IBM mainframes) and little endian (80x86 family) data.

XADD	Exchanges two operands and sums them. Used in multi-processor systems which partition algorithms across several processors.
CMPXCHG	Conditionally exchanges the contents of a register with a memory operand.
INVD	Invalidates an instruction or data cache.
WBINVD	Invalidates the cache, like INVD, but then uses an output signal to tell the secondary cache to write back the bad cache data.
INVLPG	Invalidates a matching TLB (translation lookaside buffer) entry if one is present.

Segmentation Architecture

The i486 retains the segmentation architecture of the earlier processors, but segmentation size is definable (as it is also for the 80386). Thus the 64K segments that were a problem for programmers have been eliminated, with segments being definable up to 4 GB. This is done with just a few instructions at initialization by pointing the segment registers to 00000000h and setting the size up to 4 GB. However, segmentation capability has been retained and is a real advantage for multitasking systems where each task may reside in a different segment.

Coprocessor

A coprocessor provides a number of additional instructions that can be used for math-intensive applications, such as high-precision integer functions or floating-point calculations. If these functions are performed by the main processor, the calculations might take thousands of clock cycles to perform a single complex calculation. A coprocessor will take over these functions and perform the calculations while the main processor is busy with other tasks. When the coprocessor is finished, it signals the main processor that it has the answer available.

Applications programs often are supplied in two versions, one for computers where the additional coprocessor has been installed, and one version where the main processor must do all the calculations. Other software automatically tests for the presence of a coprocessor and uses the appropriate part of the program to perform the calculations. The i486 includes a built-in functional equivalent of the 80387 coprocessor, so this costly feature is now standard with any EISA computer that uses the i486 processor.

The coprocessor offers significant advantages when using any computer-aided design, engineering, or manufacturing application. In addition, programs that perform a large number of complex mathematical calculations, such as fractal-generation programs, make extensive use of a coprocessor. The coprocessor performs the mathematical functions while the main processor performs other functions.

Summary

The i486 is basically an 80386, an 80387, and a cache memory on one chip. This results in significantly improved ease of design and performance. In addition, Intel has improved the internal architecture to allow commonly executed instructions to execute much faster. Add to that the improved clock speeds of 25 and 33 MHz, and much faster ones to come, and the i486 promises to be the heart of extremely powerful computers for a long time.

Glossary

ACK   Acknowledge.

Active high   Signal that must go to a logic high (1) to produce an effect.

Active low   Signal that must go to a logic low (0) to produce an effect.

Application Programs   Software that performs specific tasks, such as word processors, spreadsheets, and data bases.

Architecture   A term that defines the relationship between the various components and designs that make up a computer design.

Attribute   The characteristic of a pixel or character on the screen that defines its color or intensity. The Attribute information is the data stored in the video RAM memory at each location corresponding to a pixel or character location on the screen.

BCD   Binary Coded Decimal.

BIOS   Basic Input/Output System. BIOS is the program stored in the ROM BIOS that provides the software interface between the hardware and system software and application programs.

Bit The smallest unit of data that a computer can manipulate. Its state may be either on (1) or off (0), and it is usually combined with seven other bits to form a byte of data. Bits are often used to record the state of flags or the result of a register operation. The microprocessor has many instructions to support this.

BPS Bits per second.

Byte Eight bits, or binary states. Typically, a byte is typically used to store a single ASCII character, or a binary value from 0 (all bits are 0) to 255 (all bits are 1).

Cache memory Memory that stores frequently accessed data from a disk controller or main memory, used to increase processing speed.

Call Occurs when a program, typically an application program, puts certain information into the CPU registers, then "calls" (jumps to) a specified location. The program code at that location then takes the information in the registers and, based on the information, performs a task or stores the data.

Checksum byte A byte containing the eight least-significant bits of the sum of a block of code or data.

Checksum An error-checking technique used to verify a block of code or data. It is calculated by adding all of the bytes in the specified block, the sum of which forms the checksum. Subsequent adding of the bytes in the block and comparing the result against the previously calculated value is a determination of the validity of the specified block.

CMOS RAM Random-access memory that is powered by a battery when the computer is turned off. Data, such as the system configuration and other ISA and EISA parameters, is stored in the CMOS RAM.

Coprocessor A processor that works in conjunction with the CPU. On the 80486, the coprocessor is built into the 80486.

CPU Central Processing Unit. Typically, used to refer to the microprocessor, such as an 80486 or 80386, that is used in a computer system. However, some manufacturers also use the term CPU to refer to the circuit board that contains the microprocessor. Occasionally, manufacturers also use the term to refer to the computer as a whole, typically in the context of differentiating it from peripherals such as the printer or a terminal.

CTS   Clear To Send. This signal is output by the modem or printer to the computer to indicate that the modem may send data to the computer, or the printer may return status information.

DCD   Data Carrier Detect. This signal, sent by a modem to a terminal or computer, indicates that the modem has received a carrier signal from a modem on the far end of the telephone line.

DIN   Acronym for Deutsche Industrie Normenausschuss, a West German association that sets electrical standards.

Direct memory access   A means for boards or devices on the memory bus to obtain access to the main memory, and transfer data, without using the central processing unit.

DMA   See direct memory access.

DSR   Data Set Ready. Signal sent from the modem to the computer or terminal indicating that the modem is ready to be used. Typically, this signal indicates that the modem has power applied and has successfully performed its initialization (internal setup) routines.

DTR   Data Terminal Ready. Signal sent from the computer (or terminal) to the modem, indicating that the computer is ready to be used. Typically, this signal indicates that the computer has power applied.

Dword   A dword is a double word containing 2 words, or 4 bytes. With the power of the 80486 and the EISA bus, dword operations are often used to move data quickly over the 32-bit data bus.

Dynamic RAM   Dynamic Random Access Memory. Also known as Main Memory, Memory, RAM, System Memory, or System RAM.

EISA   Extended Industry Standard Architecture. Mnemonic for the new architecture about which this book is written. EISA is an enhancement of the ISA architecture (see ISA).

EGA   Enhanced Graphics Adapter.

GB   Gigabyte. 1,073,741,824 bytes.

Graphic display mode A video display mode where all positions on the screen are addressed as pixels.

Handshaking A process whereby the computer and a peripheral, such as a printer or modem, tell each other their status. This status may typically represent information such as "I am out of paper" (from a printer) or "I am ready to send" (from a computer).

Hardware interrupts Requests for attention of the CPU, and subsequent processing of code, that are generated by the hardware.

Hexadecimal Numbers expressed in base 16. Hexadecimal digits are represented by the numbers 0-9 and letters A-F. In this book, hexadecimal numbers are indicated with a lowercase h as their last character (17h).

Interrupt May be of two kinds, either hardware or software. A hardware interrupt occurs when a signal line from an interrupt controller or other similar device goes active, forcing the CPU to stop what it is doing and respond to the interrupt. This process is the result of a hardware, or signal, action. A software interrupt occurs when a program executes an INT instruction. This forces the CPU to jump to a specified location and execute a routine (small program) at that location.

ISA (Industry Standard Architecture) A bus and computer architecture compatible with IBM AT personal computers.

K Kilobytes. 1,024 bytes.

MB MegaByte. 1,048,576 bytes.

MDA Monochrome Display Adapter.

Monochrome A display with a single color, normally green or amber, though white is sometimes used.

NMI Non-Maskable Interrupt, typically used to report error conditions. This interrupt is normally found at interrupt vector 02h.

Operating system The software that interfaces the applications program to the computer hardware. The operating system interfaces between input and output functions, data files, program files, and system memory. Examples of operating systems are MS-DOS, OS/2, or UNIX.

Palette The set of all the possible colors a Video Display Adapter can produce.

Pixel   A dot on the screen in the graphics modes.

Processor interrupts   Interrupts generated by the processor, typically in response to error conditions.

Protective ground   Chassis ground for the computer, the printer, or the modem. This line ties the grounds together to reduce the possibility of shock.

RAM   Random Access Memory. This type of memory is used for general storage of the computer's programs and data. It can be either read or written to, although it will lose its contents when the power is turned off. (Also see ROM)

Register   A latch in the 80386 or 80486 that stores information or controls a function. For example, a register may contain data to be sent out to a port, or an address where the processor has stored information, or an address where the processor should go to get the next instruction to be processed.

RGB   A mnemonic for Red-Green-Blue. These are the three primary colors used in a color display. In a typical VGA display, these are varied in intensity and combination to produce all the possible colors which can be displayed.

RI   Ring Indicator. This signal, sent by a modem to a terminal or computer, indicates that there is a phone call coming in. This signal is the electrical equivalent of the telephone ringing. When the computer receives this signal, it usually activates (through an interrupt) the program or routines to answer incoming calls.

ROM   Read Only Memory. This type of computer memory can only be read by the processor, not written to. ROM-type memory typically contains the BIOS code or utilities that must be accessible even when the computer has no disk drives attached from which to load the operating system. ROM memory retains its contents even when the power is removed. (Also see RAM)

Routine   A piece of a program that performs a single and specific function. For example, a routine might output a character to a parallel port. The program would put the character into one of the CPU's registers, and then the "output routine" would be called. This output routine would then read the character in the CPU's register and send it to the printer. The routine would then return to the program which called it, to repeat the process, or if all the characters had been sent, to continue on with the program.

RTS   Ready To Send. This signal is output by the computer to a modem or printer to indicate that the computer is ready to send data.

RXD   Receive Data. This is the data signal that is being received from an other piece of equipment. On the other end, this signal is the TXD (Transmit Data) signal.

SG   Signal Ground. This is the ground reference for the various signals transmitted on the RS232 cable. Although under normal conditions (in a 25-pin connector only), SG (Signal Ground) may be the same as the PG (Protective Ground) signal, this is not always the case. These two signals, SG and PG, should never be tied together in the cable. They may be tied in the equipment by design of the engineer. The protective ground signal (Pin 1 in a 25 pin connector) does not appear in a 9-pin connector.

Software interrupts   Interrupts generated by the INT "n" instruction.

TSR   Terminate and Stay Ready. This type of program is loaded into the computer's memory and then seems to disappear. It becomes active when, typically, a hot key is pressed that calls the program up.

TXD   Transmit Data. This is the actual data signal being transmitted from one piece of equipment to another. On the other end this signal is the RXD (Receive Data) signal, and is connected to the RXD pin of that connector.

VGA   Video Graphics Adapter. This is the high-resolution video display card that is found on most of the EISA computers. Other video display cards are the EGA, CGA, and MDA.

Video attributes   The video characteristics of alphanumeric characters displayed on the CRT. Video attributes include reverse video, blinking, underline, and high intensity.

Word   A word is 16 binary bits, made up of two 8-bit bytes. Word-sized data transfers are often found in 16-bit computers to double the speed with which data can be moved. (Earlier personal computers transferred data a byte (8 bits) at a time.) Note that 8-bit data transfer is still used in transferring data to most serial and parallel I/O devices.

Appendix

7-Bit ASCII Reference Chart

Dec	ASCII	Octal	Hex	Binary	Definition
0	NUL	000	00	0000000	^@ (used for padding) <NULL>
1	SOH	001	01	0000001	^A (start of header)
2	STX	002	02	0000010	^B (start of text)
3	ETX	003	03	0000011	^C (end of text)
4	EOT	004	04	0000100	^D (end of transmission)
5	ENQ	005	05	0000101	^E (enquiry)
6	ACK	006	06	0000110	^F (acknowledge)
7	BEL	007	07	0000111	^G (bell or alarm) <BELL>
8	BS	010	08	0001000	^H (backspace) <BS>
9	HT	011	09	0001001	^I (horizontal tab) <TAB>
10	LF	012	0A	0001010	^J (line feed) <LF>
11	VT	013	0B	0001011	^K (vertical tab)
12	FF	014	0C	0001100	^L (form feed, new page)

13	CR	015	0D	0001101	^M (carriage return) <CR>
14	SO	016	0E	0001110	^N (shift out)
15	SI	017	0F	0001111	^O (shift in)
16	DLE	020	10	0010000	^P (data link escape)
17	DC1	021	11	0010001	^Q (device control 1, XON)
18	DC2	022	12	0010010	^R (device control 2)
19	DC3	023	13	0010011	^S (device control 3, XOFF)
20	DC4	024	14	0010100	^T (device control 4)
21	NAK	025	15	0010101	^U (negative acknowledge)
22	SYN	026	16	0010110	^V (synchronous idle)
23	ETB	027	17	0010111	^W (end transmission block)
24	CAN	030	18	0011000	^X (cancel)
25	EM	031	19	0011001	^Y (end of medium)
26	SUB	032	1A	0011010	^Z (substitute)
27	ESC	033	1B	0011011	^[(escape, alter mode, SEL)
28	FS	034	1C	0011100	^\ (file separator)
29	GS	035	1D	0011101	^] (group separator)
30	RS	036	1E	0011110	^^ (record separator)
31	US	037	1F	0011111	^_ (unit separator)
32	SP	040	20	0100000	space or blank <SP>
33	!	041	21	0100001	exclamation mark
34	"	042	22	0100010	double quote
35	#	043	23	0100011	number sign, pound sign
36	$	044	24	0100100	dollar sign
37	%	045	25	0100101	percent sign
38	&	046	26	0100110	ampersand sign
39	'	047	27	0100111	apostrophe
40	(	050	28	0101000	left parenthesis
41	)	051	29	0101001	right parenthesis
42	*	052	2A	0101010	asterisk (star)
43	+	053	2B	0101011	plus sign
44	,	054	2C	0101100	comma
45	−	055	2D	0101101	minus sign (dash)
46	.	056	2E	0101110	period (decimal point)

47	/	057	2F	0101111	(right) slash
48	0	060	30	0110000	number zero
49	1	061	31	0110001	number one
50	2	062	32	0110010	number two
51	3	063	33	0110011	number three
52	4	064	34	0110100	number four
53	5	065	35	0110101	number five
54	6	066	36	0110110	number six
55	7	067	37	0110111	number seven
56	8	070	38	0111000	number eight
57	9	071	39	0111001	number nine
58	:	072	3A	0111010	colon
59	;	073	3B	0111011	semicolon
60	<	074	3C	0111100	less-than sign
61	=	075	3D	0111101	equal sign
62	>	076	3E	0111110	greater-than sign
63	?	077	3F	0111111	question mark
64	@	100	40	1000000	at sign
65	A	101	41	1000001	upper-case letter A
66	B	102	42	1000010	upper-case letter B
67	C	103	43	1000011	upper-case letter C
68	D	104	44	1000100	upper-case letter D
69	E	105	45	1000101	upper-case letter E
70	F	106	46	1000110	upper-case letter F
71	G	107	47	1000111	upper-case letter G
72	H	110	48	1001000	upper-case letter H
73	I	111	49	1001001	upper-case letter I
74	J	112	4A	1001010	upper-case letter J
75	K	113	4B	1001011	upper-case letter K
76	L	114	4C	1001100	upper-case letter L
77	M	115	4D	1001101	upper-case letter M
78	N	116	4E	1001110	upper-case letter N
79	O	117	4F	1001111	upper-case letter O
80	P	120	50	1010000	upper-case letter P

81	Q	121	51	1010001	upper-case letter Q
82	R	122	52	1010010	upper-case letter R
83	S	123	53	1010011	upper-case letter S
84	T	124	54	1010100	upper-case letter T
85	U	125	55	1010101	upper-case letter U
86	V	126	56	1010110	upper-case letter V
87	W	127	57	1010111	upper-case letter W
88	X	130	58	1011000	upper-case letter X
89	Y	131	59	1011001	upper-case letter Y
90	Z	132	5A	1011010	upper-case letter Z
91	[	133	5B	1011011	left square bracket
92	\	134	5C	1011100	left slash (backslash)
93	]	135	5D	1011101	right square bracket
94	^	136	5E	1011110	up arrow (carat)
95	_	137	5F	1011111	underscore
96	`	140	60	1100000	back quote
97	a	141	61	1100001	lower-case letter a
98	b	142	62	1100010	lower-case letter b
99	c	143	63	1100011	lower-case letter c
100	d	144	64	1100100	lower-case letter d
101	e	145	65	1100101	lower-case letter e
102	f	146	66	1100110	lower-case letter f
103	g	147	67	1100111	lower-case letter g
104	h	150	68	1101000	lower-case letter h
105	i	151	69	1101001	lower-case letter i
106	j	152	6A	1101010	lower-case letter j
107	k	153	6B	1101011	lower-case letter k
108	l	154	6C	1101100	lower-case letter l
109	m	155	6D	1101101	lower-case letter m
110	n	156	6E	1101110	lower-case letter n
111	o	157	6F	1101111	lower-case letter o
112	p	160	70	1110000	lower-case letter p
113	q	161	71	1110001	lower-case letter q
114	r	162	72	1110010	lower-case letter r

115	s	163	73	1110011	lower-case letter s
116	t	164	74	1110100	lower-case letter t
117	u	165	75	1110101	lower-case letter u
118	v	166	76	1110110	lower-case letter v
119	w	167	77	1110111	lower-case letter w
120	x	170	78	1111000	lower-case letter x
121	y	171	79	1111001	lower-case letter y
122	z	172	7A	1111010	lower-case letter z
123	{	173	7B	1111011	left curly brace
124	|	174	7C	1111100	vertical bar
125	}	175	7D	1111101	right curly brace
126	~	176	7E	1111110	tilde
127	DEL	177	7F	1111111	delete, rub out

Index

227

Tildes (˜) for active low states, 4
Time command (DOS), 47
Transmit Buffer register, serial port,
    173–174
Tree program (DOS), 41, 48
TXD (Transmit Data) RS232 signal,
    162, 164, 166, 168
Type A DMA cycles, 72–73
Type B DMA cycles, 73
Type command (DOS), 48

Underline attribute, VGA, 148
Underline Location register, VGA,
    136
Unlock function (system
    configuration), 88
UPDATE overlay function, 112
Update phase for overlay files, 101
Utility programs, 38
Utility signals, 62–63

Ver command (DOS), 48
Verify command (DOS), 48
Verify function (system
    configuration), 88
Version, DOS, 48
Vertical Display Enable End register,
    VGA, 136
Vertical Retrace End register, VGA,
    135–136
Vertical Retrace Start register, VGA,
    135
Vertical Total register, VGA, 132
VGA (Video Graphics Array), 121–
    122
    attribute controller registers for,
        142–144

BIOS functions with, 145–151, 154–
    156
components for, 123–124
CRT controller registers for, 130–
    138
external registers for, 125–127
graphics controller registers for,
    138–142
modes of operation for, 123
programming examples for, 151–156
programming of, 124
sequencer registers for, 127–130
video board for, 98–99
Video
    compatibility for, 121–122
    connector for, 122
    DOS 4 support for, 39, 41
    memory for, 20
    See also VGA (Video Graphics
        Array)
View menu (system configuration),
    88–89
Virtual drives, 47
Vol command (DOS), 46, 48
Volume labels, 46

WBINVD instruction (i486), 212
Write Character and Attribute
    function, VGA, 147
Write Character Only function, VGA,
    147–148
Write String function, VGA, 149–150
Write TTY function, VGA, 149

XADD instruction (i486), 212
Xcopy program (DOS), 48
XMIT BIOS function, 183

This book may be kept